Social Policy

Hartley Dean

polity

First published in 2006 by Polity Press

Reprinted 2006

Polity Press
65 Bridge Street
Cambridge CB2 1UR, UK.

Polity Press
350 Main Street
Malden, MA 02148, USA

ISBN-10: 0-7456-3434-6
ISBN-10: 0-7456-3435-4 (pb)
ISBN-13: 978-0-7456-3434-0
ISBN-13: 978-0-7456-3435-7 (pb)

A catalogue record for this book is available from the British Library.

Typeset in 10 on 12 pt Sabon
by SNP Best-set Typesetter Ltd., Hong Kong
Printed and bound in Great Britain by T.J. International Ltd. Padstow Cornwall

For further information on Polity, visit our website: www.polity.co.uk

For Pam

Contents

Figures and Tables

Figures

Tables

Boxes

Preface

This book will, I hope, do exactly what it says on the cover. It will provide a short introduction to the subject of Social Policy (with a capital 'S' and a capital 'P'). In the process, it will also touch upon some aspects of the social policy or policies (with a small 's' and a small 'p') by which a variety of governmental and other organizations throughout the world attend to, promote, neglect or undermine our wellbeing. But its purpose is to serve as an introduction, not as a comprehensive textbook. It will identify key issues, but it cannot and will not explore them in any great detail. It will explain past, present and future trends in general terms, but it will contain few of the kinds of facts and figures that tend to go rapidly out of date. It will identify some of the most important or helpful literature sources, both classic and contemporary, but it will not contain exhaustive bibliographic references. I aim, as simply as I can, to convey my own passion for Social Policy as a field of study.

Passion is a strong word: a bit 'over the top' you might think. Let me therefore explain how I discovered Social Policy. When I left university with a generic degree in 'Social Science', I went to work at an independent advice centre in Brixton in inner south London. Brixton is known, on the one hand, for its cosmopolitan multi-ethnic community and, on the other, for the extent of the poverty that exists there in the midst of big city affluence. Sadly, it is also remembered for the riots that happened in the summer of 1981. I worked there for twelve exciting and eventful years (including the period in which the riots took place). In that time I became an expert on all sorts of things to do with social security, housing, education, health and social care. I became fascinated by the ways in which it is, or ought to be, possible to make systematic provision to meet diverse human needs. In the course of the battles with authority that I fought with and for people in Brixton I also became increasingly angry: angry, because systems that were supposed to help people often failed or, worse still, hindered or controlled them. I retreated to academia to try and find out why that was; to make sense of what I had been doing. I discovered that the things I had been learning about and the many questions I was asking were all central elements of a subject called Social Policy.

The attraction for Social Policy, for me, is that it is a subject with few, if any, boundaries. It is relevant to every facet of our lives. It is genuinely multi-disciplinary. It reaches beyond the febrile controversies of everyday politics to grasp critically at underlying issues and injustices. It is outward looking, encompassing both the global and the local; the universal and the personal. In the ten short chapters that follow I start in chapter 1 by explaining the scope and importance of Social Policy; in chapters 2 and 3, I discuss its foundations and contemporary significance; in chapters 4, 5 and 6 I explore the principal issues it addresses and their economic, political and sociological dimensions; in chapters 8 and 9 I address some of the fundamental challenges it faces; and, finally, in chapter 10 I consider its future.

The book has been written as an invitation to potential students of Social Policy and for students who are new to the subject. It may also, however, be of interest to colleagues and to academics from both inside and outside the subject, because there is a sense in which I am attempting here to refresh our understanding of how Social Policy may be approached. I present the subject positively as the study of human well-being. I do so not because this is the only approach that may be taken, but because I am persuaded that it is the most attractive way of introducing the subject to new or potential students.

Social Policy has, until relatively recently, been a peculiarly British academic subject and, insofar as I am an English academic working in an English university, several of the illustrations on which I draw will relate to English or UK social policies. Given the breadth of the subject and the brevity of the book I have made these examples very general and kept their number to a minimum. Social Policy is about real life and, in the classroom, one way to bring it alive is through real life case studies and the sharing of everyday experiences. But in view of the complexity and diversity of real lives and the wide audience at which this short introduction is aimed I have been mindful of the risk that even the most carefully chosen illustrative materials may appear parochial or puzzling to some readers. This, therefore, is where the reader's own imagination must come into play. To get the best out of this book, you are invited to apply the ideas, concepts and arguments that I shall outline to your own life and experiences; to your own concerns and beliefs. For those of you who take up that invitation, you will discover that this is a vital element in the study of Social Policy.

This is meant to be a book for anybody who might be interested in Social Policy, whatever they are doing and wherever in the world they find themselves. A book of this length can only scratch the surface, but I hope it will reveal something of the vibrancy, diversity and humanity that lies beneath.

Hartley Dean
London School of Economics and Political Science

Acknowledgements

All sorts of people have contributed to the thinking that went into the writing of this short book. They are too many to enumerate, but that doesn't mean I am not grateful. If you have ever discussed the meaning of Social Policy with me, you have probably had an influence in some way or at some point.

I must, however, specifically acknowledge my considerable gratitude to those who kindly took the time and trouble to read and comment on earlier drafts or some or all of these chapters, namely Catherine and Hugh Bochell, Pam Dean, Bill Jordan, Eileen Munro and David Piachaud. They have all offered valuable advice and, where I have heeded it, I'm sure it will have enhanced the offering I now present. If, out of stubbornness or misjudgement, I ignored their advice, and whenever there is error, deficiency or confusion in the pages that follow, it is I alone who am to blame. I am also especially grateful to Louise Knight from Polity Press for encouraging me to write this book in the first place and Ellen McKinlay, Helen Gray and Gail Ferguson for so ably handling its production.

1

What *is* Social Policy?

When I tell people I teach Social Policy, a fairly common response is 'Oh! . . . *[pause]*. What's that exactly?' Social Policy textbooks sometimes try and suggest that Social Policy is hard to define. Or else they contend there is something 'confusing' about the distinction to be drawn between Social Policy as an academic subject on the one hand and the specific outcomes of the social policy-making process on the other; or about whether Social Policy is 'merely' an interdisciplinary field of study, as opposed to a social science discipline in its own right (Alcock 2003). For my part, however, I don't find the question difficult at all. Social Policy is the study of human wellbeing, to which there can be two kinds of response:

- So it's all about *doing good* for people?
- So it must be about pretty much *everything* really?

The answer to both comments is 'Well, yes and no'. More specifically, Social Policy entails the study of the social relations necessary for human wellbeing and the systems by which wellbeing may be promoted. It's about the many and various things that affect the kinds of life that you and I and everyone can live. My preference, incidentally, is for the term 'wellbeing', rather than 'welfare', because wellbeing is about how well people *are*, not how well they *do* (which, strictly speaking, is what welfare means). Think for a moment about the things you need to make life worth living: essential services, such as healthcare and education; a means of livelihood, such as a job and money; vital but intangible things, such as love and security. Now think about the ways in which these can be organized: by government and official bodies; through businesses, social groups, charities, local associations and churches; through neighbours, families and loved ones. Understanding these things is the stuff of Social Policy.

In this chapter I aim to illustrate, first, the immense scale of the phenomena with which Social Policy is concerned, but also its quite specific nature; second, the fabulous diversity of the social scientific traditions on which Social Policy can draw, but also the strict rigour of its focus; third, the relevance of Social Policy to everybody's individual, everyday lives; but fourth, the importance of Social Policy to human society in general.

Before I begin, however, let me return just for one moment to the 'confusion' alluded to above between Social Policy, the subject, and the social policy or policies that are the object of our study. As I have already signalled in my Preface, I propose throughout this book to adopt a rather simple convention that is not in general use, but which may, I hope, allay confusion. When I refer to Social Policy with a capital 'S' and a capital 'P', I am writing about the academic study of social policy. When I refer to social policy with a lower-case 's' and a lower-case 'p', I shall be talking about the general or the particular policy or policies that have been determined in the fields of social security, health, education, social care and protection or – as you will see – in any number of spheres that may bear upon human wellbeing.

Hey, Big Spender!

Social Policy is concerned with much, much more than the things that governments spend our money on. Nevertheless, though it refers only to the visible tip of the Social Policy iceberg, the most conspicuous evidence of the importance of social policies is 'social spending'. If we take a country such as the UK, the government planned in the 2004–5 tax year to spend roughly £320 billion on what may conventionally be defined as 'social' or social policy spending (HM Treasury 2004a); that is to say, on things like pensions, hospitals and schools. That amounts to about two thirds of total public spending and around one quarter of this particular nation's annual income (or what is usually called Gross Domestic Product or 'GDP'). It is a huge sum of money: more than most people can really comprehend or even imagine. If one were searching for a comparison, £320 billion is over seven and a half thousand times more than the first ever double rollover jackpot on the UK National Lottery, which was 'only' £42 million, but is still perhaps more than any ordinary person could really envisage owning, let alone spending. What spends on social policy is hardly small change!

And yet, the UK is by no means exceptional. In fact, as a pro of GDP the UK's social policy spending is rather less than in a other developed countries. In countries like France and Germa..y, for example, social policy spending is equivalent to rather more than one quarter of GDP, while in Sweden it is as much as one third (see, for example, Taylor-Gooby 2002: table 1). There are, on the other hand, other major countries where social spending is proportionately much lower than in the UK. In the USA, for example, it is equivalent to barely one sixth of GDP. And, of course, many developing countries can afford to spend very little on social policy at all. In chapter 3 we shall try to understand a bit more about the differences between different countries' approaches to social policy.

Also, the amount governments spend on social policy can go up or down, depending on changing priorities. In democratic countries such priorities will to some extent reflect the wishes of the electorate and the taxpayers who must finance such spending. But it depends just as much on the fluctuating needs of the population and on the state of the country's economy. To take the UK as an example once again, the extent of its social spending had grown from around 2 per cent of GDP at the very beginning of the twentieth century to somewhere around its present level by the 1970s. Since then spending has fluctuated as Conservative governments during the 1980s and '90s attempted, in spite of a variety of pressures, to 'keep the lid on' (Glennerster 1998). Following this, Labour governments, after an initial period of restraint, have allowed social spending to increase slightly, particularly in the areas of health and education (HM Treasury 2004b). We shall try to understand a bit more about ideological, demographic and economic causes of such variations in the chapters that follow.

For the moment, however, let us focus on the scale and nature of social policy spending. Table 1.1 provides a simplified explanation of the UK government's budget plans for the year in which this book was written. The expenditure headings are very broadly defined, so the picture that is presented is rather rough and ready. None the less, this tells us that the UK government was planning to spend roughly twelve times as much on social policy as it was on defence, or on law and order. By this criterion we might say that social policy in fact receives a much higher priority than war making or crime busting.

However, table 1.1 also shows us that, for example, the government expected to spend more than eight times as much on pensions and social security benefits as on housing and the environment. In a country such as the UK, that is perhaps hardly surprising these days. The UK is quite

Table 1.1 UK government spending 2004–5 (projected)

	£ billion	% total spending	% GDP
Social spending			
Social security	138	28	12
Health	81	17	7
Education	63	13	5
Housing and environment	17	3	1
Personal social services	22	5	2
Other spending			
Defence	27	6	2
Law and order	29	6	2
Industry, agriculture and employment	20	4	2
Transport	16	3	1
Other (e.g. sport and culture international development, etc.)	49	10	4
Debt interest	25	5	2
Total public spending	**488**	**100**	**41**

The budget headings and classification of spending differ slightly from previous conventions, having been adjusted to accord with international standards. Figures may not sum to total due to rounding.
Source: http://budget2004.treasury.gov.uk/page_09.html (Crown Copyright) and see HM Treasury 2004a.

unusual compared to other countries because such a high proportion of householders (more than two thirds) own their own homes and so most spending on housing tends to be 'private', rather than 'public'. In other words, it's not that we don't as a nation spend money on housing, it's simply a question of how we organize this. In chapter 4 we shall see that although the government's social policies in respect of housing may not entail massive amounts of public *spending*, they do, for example, entail the *regulation* of housing provision.

We shall also see that although governments may spend a great deal of public money on pensions for older people, this may be more than matched by private spending on occupational and personal pension schemes, all of which, like private housing, may be closely regulated by social policy. On top of this, as we shall see in chapters 8 and 9, the definition of what does and doesn't count as a social policy or as social spending is increasingly being challenged. Social Policy is about more than the services governments provide. Even when we take account of the staggering sums of public money that are recorded as being spent on social policy, particularly in the countries of the developed world, this is still not a true indicator of the extent to which social policy may touch our lives as we grow up and grow old, as workers and as citizens, in our private lives and through the public institutions with which we engage.

None the less, in a world where money matters, Social Policy is a very substantial subject.

Butterflies versus Magpies

In the last section we adopted a very simple approach to the economics of public spending. Social Policy as an academic subject is in the habit of adopting all kinds of different approaches. That is one of its greatest attractions. It brings in ideas and analytical methods from sociology, from political science and from economics; it employs insights from social anthropology, demography, socio-legal studies, social psychology, social history, human geography and development studies; it will frequently draw upon philosophy; in fact it will go pretty much wherever it needs to find the best way to study issues relevant to the achievement of human wellbeing. What is more, Social Policy is not just multi-disciplinary, it is also inter-disciplinary. In other words it combines approaches from the different social sciences.

This may sound as if Social Policy is just a sort of 'pick-and-mix' subject; a subject that's good for people who can't make up their minds. This is not the case. Certainly, Social Policy is a wonderful subject for people who don't want to tie themselves down to just one discipline, but that doesn't mean it is suitable for ditherers, or for the kind of intellectual butterflies that flutter aimlessly from idea to idea. Students of Social Policy are more like magpies than butterflies. They are pragmatic, even ruthless, in the way they pick whatever they need from across the social sciences in order to fashion answers to real life issues. There is an element of sheer promiscuity about Social Policy in its willingness to seize upon attractive and workable ideas from across the social scientific spectrum. But it remains a highly rigorous subject because it retains a highly specific commitment to the cause of human wellbeing.

Understanding what is required to achieve human wellbeing means studying social, political and economic processes. It can entail attention to the complex details of policy design or to abstract theories and generalized overviews. It may require the ability to analyse statistical information; to evaluate the successes and failures of particular policies; to interpret popular aspirations; to investigate the perceptions of marginalized or vulnerable people; to understand the past; and to anticipate the future.

We refer to Social Policy as a social science, and the term 'science' might suggest that it is cold and clinical, hard and objective. Originally, however, the term 'science' was applied to all branches of human knowledge, including creative and philosophical forms of thinking. Social Policy is self-evidently concerned with the policy-making process, which has always entailed an element of intuition and creativity. Aneurin Bevan, the firebrand Labour politician who was responsible in the 1940s for hammering out the political compromises that established the UK's National Health Service, once said:

> By the study of anthropology, sociology, psychology and such elements of social and political economy as are relevant, we try to work out our correct principles to guide us in our approach to the social problems of the time. Nevertheless, the application of those principles to a given situation is an art. (1952: 35–6)

To my mind, this is a pretty good explanation of what Social Policy is about. Social Policy is concerned with hard evidence, technical theories and logical analysis, but it must also be creative. It often calls for imagination and insight. Social Policy is as much about feelings as about facts. To study Social Policy properly one needs commitment; one needs to be able to empathize with others; one needs to interpret the world around.

Who Cares?

This leads us to the question of why we should be concerned about the attainment of human wellbeing. Human societies are complex associations of interdependent beings. In other words, human beings are social creatures who depend upon each other. Early sociologists, such as Emile Durkheim (1893), endeavoured to understand the complexity of modern societies in terms of the increasingly sophisticated ways in which people collaborate to produce life's necessities. The social policies to which societies give birth may be understood as the way in which any particular society recognizes and gives expression to the interdependency of its members. Writing in the same era as Aneurin Bevan, an academic and founding father of Social Policy, Richard Titmuss, argued that what we have come to know as the 'welfare state' was then emerging because

> . . . more 'states of dependency' have been defined and recognised as collective responsibilities, and more differential provision has been

> made in respect of them. These 'states of dependency' arise for the vast majority of the population whenever they are not in a position to 'earn life' for themselves and their families; they are then dependent people. In industrialised societies, there are many causes of dependency; they may be 'natural' dependencies as in childhood, extreme old age and child-bearing. They may be caused by physical and psychological ill health and incapacity; in part, these are culturally determined dependencies. Or they may be wholly or predominantly determined by social and cultural factors. These, it may be said, are the 'man-made' dependencies. (1955: 64)

Since Titmuss wrote these words the world has moved on. In the age of information technologies, most industrialized societies are better described as 'post-industrialized'. The so-called 'golden age' of the welfare state – which was dawning as Titmuss wrote – may now already have passed (see Esping-Andersen 1996: ch. 1). None the less, though they may be reluctant to admit it (see Dean 2004a: ch. 4) people are still as interdependent as ever they were. The ways in which we meet our welfare needs may have been changing, but the welfare state – as we have seen above – is still very much in evidence in most developed nations of the world. And Titmuss was right. Many of the dependencies we experience are fashioned by social and cultural factors: for example, by changes in the nature of labour markets and by changing patterns of household formation. The way we can or can't depend on jobs and our families is forever changing and this in turn affects how we might depend on the wider community or on the state.

Titmuss has relevance for another reason. In a later work (Titmuss 1970), he drew on social anthropological evidence to suggest that pre-industrial societies were based on gift giving. The interdependency of the members of supposedly 'primitive' societies could be sustained through an array of unilateral transactions or gift-relationships. The function of social policies in advanced capitalist societies, according to Titmuss, is to perpetuate such gift-relationships. In an age when societies are more complex, more differentiated and most transactions take the form of bilateral market exchanges, a system of taxes, benefits and public services enables us to give to one another: not just to our immediate neighbours, but also, importantly, to distant and anonymous strangers. Not only is it still possible to sustain the interdependent nature of our human existence, but – in theory at least – it is possible through the development of social policies to compensate for some of the 'person-made' or manufactured dependencies that contemporary society generates.

This might make it sound as if social policies are simply a vehicle for human altruism. If this were so, Social Policy, by implication, would be a rather warm-hearted, 'cuddly' sort of academic subject. There is, however, more to it than that: first, because our dependencies are inevitably bound up within unequal relations of power; second, because the ethical basis of social policy provision, or 'giving', are inevitably contested.

Compensating individuals for their dependency may entail making material provision for them at various stages in their lives, but it can also entail protecting them against the exploitation that may be associated with particular kinds of dependency. Most people would agree that society should protect children and older people from child or elder abuse and policies to this end are by and large uncontroversial. We are all against sin! However, the idea that we should protect workers from exploitation by their employers raises issues to do with class and class conflict. Social policies may to a greater or lesser extent enable workers to avoid dependency on an employer other than upon socially acceptable terms (e.g. Esping-Andersen 1990): this is more controversial. There are other forms of dependency which social policies in developed welfare states have not only ignored or failed to address, but may have perpetuated. Of particular concern is women's dependency within families and issues of gender inequality. Social policies can be framed in ways that either reinforce or refashion social assumptions about who should care for whom and in what ways. These are issues to which we shall return in chapter 7, but the point for now is that Social Policy is concerned with the different ways in which – with or without a welfare state – we as human beings care for and about each other.

The distinction between 'caring for' and 'caring about' (see Parker 1981) is an important one. 'Caring for' is a practical business and most of it, even in developed welfare states, is undertaken within families and by women. Responsibility for caring for children, for sick, disabled or frail elderly people tends to fall, in the first instance at least, upon mothers and female family members. 'Caring about', on the other hand, is something that can be addressed through, or consigned to, the public sphere of social policy making. The public policy-making sphere is generally male dominated and its ethos is informed, not by the nature of human relationships, but by abstract principles concerning the importance of Work, Family and Nation (Williams 1989). Such principles have tended in many welfare states to accord rights selectively to white male working breadwinners, at the expense, it has been argued, of women, disabled people, minority ethnic groups and foreigners. Certain feminists have argued that social policies should be founded on a different ethos (e.g. Sevenhuijssen 2000), an approach that would start from the idea that we are all – men and women alike – equally interdependent and equally capable of caring for one another. This opens up new ways of thinking about the relevance of policy to our everyday lives – for example, about the relative importance of care work, as opposed to paid work. But as societies become ever more differentiated and the world as a whole becomes ever more dynamically interconnected, we also need to rethink some of those abstract principles by which we define and care about the rights of strangers, of excluded minorities and of distant peoples (see Dean 2004a: ch. 10).

The role of Social Policy, as a critical academic subject, is to engage with such debates and to reflect on the scope and the attainable limits of the pursuit of human wellbeing.

A Good Life

This brings us finally in this introductory chapter to say something about what 'wellbeing' might entail. The term 'refers to the totality of an individual's social relations' (Hoggett 2000: 145). Over 2,000 years ago, long before the arguably charming but wholly facile BBC television comedy series bearing a similar title, Aristotle sought to define what is required to live 'a good life'. His answer, according to Alberto – the mysterious philosophy teacher in Jostein Gaarder's novel, *Sophie's World* – was that:

> Man can only achieve happiness by using all his abilities and capabilities. Aristotle held that there are three forms of happiness. The first . . . is a life of pleasure and enjoyment. The second . . . is a life as a free and responsible citizen. The third . . . is a life as a thinker and philosopher. Aristotle then emphasized that all three criteria must be present for man to find happiness and fulfilment. (Gaarder 1996: 97)

Shockingly, by current standards, Aristotle considered that neither women nor slaves were capable of achieving the virtues required for a good life. Such virtues, it would appear, were available only to mature male citizens of the Athenian city-state. Despite this, there is a holistic neo-Aristotelian notion of wellbeing that remains influential today. In particular, one of the foremost philosophers of our present era, Amartya Sen, has developed the concept of capabilities. It may be inferred from the quotation above that there is a distinction to be drawn between 'abilities' and 'capabilities'. Sen uses the term 'capabilities' to refer not simply to what people are able to do, but to their freedom to choose and to lead the kind of lives they value – and have reason to value (see, for example, Sen 1985; 1999). Sen has employed this concept in a way that is important for Social Policy because it cuts through the debate about whether our human needs are absolute or culturally relative; whether, that is, all humans have certain irreducible needs, or whether we tend merely to want the things that others have in the society in which we happen to live. Sen's argument is that our need for commodities is relative: it depends entirely on the social and economic context in which we find ourselves, but our need for capabilities – for the freedom properly to function as members of human society – is absolute. Poverty, for Sen, should be defined in terms of 'capability deprivation'.

Sen's approach has influenced the development of a particular theory of human need, espoused by Len Doyal and Ian Gough (1991). In opposition to those who argue that it is impossible to define basic human needs, they insist there are universal preconditions for participation in a good life that are applicable to all human beings. These are defined as physical health and personal autonomy. Not only do we need to be healthy enough physically to survive, but as human beings we also need to be able to make informed choices about our lives. Although these basic needs can be met in a multitude of different ways, it is possible nevertheless to define certain 'universal satisfier characteristics' or intermediate needs, namely adequate nutritional food and water, adequate protective housing, non-hazardous work and physical environments, appropriate healthcare, security in childhood, significant primary relationships, physical and economic security, safe birth control and childbearing, and appropriate basic and cross-cultural education.

The 'needs satisfiers' that Doyal and Gough identify would guarantee a dignified, if potentially a rather frugal, existence. It should be emphasized, however, that this is a theory with a 'normative' purpose. Not only does it say this is how we can scientifically define what human beings need, it is also saying that this is how we define the societal preconditions for *optimizing* the satisfaction of human needs. A similar kind of neo-Aristotelian argument is developed by Martha Nussbaum (2000) who has written about what she calls 'combined capabilities': the idea that individual capabilities may be facilitated by institutional conditions; or, in other words, by social policies.

We must always be mindful that social policies, when they are implemented, do not necessarily promote human capabilities or well-being. They can also undermine them. As we shall see in chapter 8, the study of Social Policy must contend with the reality that social policies often have a 'dark side' (e.g. Squires 1990). On the one hand, ensuring that some of us have a good life may necessarily mean that we must protect ourselves from the predations of 'others', whose criminal or antisocial behaviour we may seek to curtail. In this context, criminal justice policies – and their consequences both for the victims and the perpetrators of crime – are a necessary concern of Social Policy. But beyond the realms of criminal justice policy there are many social policies that impose rules or conditions upon the day-to-day behaviour of all kinds of people: rules and conditions that may, for example, enforce particular interpretations of work and family responsibility. In the process, social policies, intentionally or unintentionally, may stigmatize, exclude or control certain individuals or groups and so deny them the personal autonomy that is necessary to human wellbeing. As a critical social science subject, Social Policy is concerned with the extent to which social policies succeed or fail to promote human wellbeing and with their potentially counterproductive effects.

It remains the case, therefore, that Social Policy is about how people may achieve a good life. This does not entail making everyone happy, which isn't feasible given that life and death entail pain as well as pleasure. Nor does it mean turning us all into philosophers, which seems hardly desirable given that human beings are diverse in their interests and propensities. What it does entail is the systematic study of how societies of different kinds can ensure, so far as possible, that their members enjoy good health, that they can freely participate in society and that they are able to think for themselves.

During the student protests in Paris in 1968, street posters appeared bearing the slogan 'Be realistic: demand the impossible'. Defining Social Policy in the terms I have suggested is aspirational and, in one sense, revolutionary: it is demanding the impossible. In another sense, however, it is perfectly sensible and strictly pragmatic: it is, indeed, wholly realistic. There is no mystery to the paradox. It is simply that Social Policy is a subject that allows its students to address some of the biggest questions to do with the nature of our social existence, but in practically relevant ways.

Summary

This chapter has explained that the subject, Social Policy, involves the study of human wellbeing, the social relations necessary for wellbeing and the systems by which wellbeing may be promoted:

- It is concerned, in part, with the social policies that governments have in relation to such things as social security, health, education, housing and the personal social services. In the developed countries of the world, the scale of spending on social policies is absolutely massive and generally accounts for a major slice of national income.
- It is both multi- and inter-disciplinary. It is not, however, a subject for butterflies – who flit aimlessly from idea to idea – but for magpies,

who purposefully, but imaginatively, pick what they need from across the social sciences in a way that is both pragmatic and creative.

- It focuses on the nature of human interdependency; on the way in which people care for and about each other; on the part the 'welfare state' plays in shaping the nature of caring – and, for example, the gender implications; on ethical questions about principles of care and justice.
- Its goal is to maximize people's chances of a good life. Its substance, therefore, lies in the theoretical debate and practical definition of what constitutes the good life and the fundamental nature of human need.

2

Where did it Come From?

Social Policy crystallized as an academic subject relatively recently (see, for example, Bulmer et al. 1989). It emerged primarily because the social policies that are its object of study had by then become a distinctive, important and contested terrain, worthy of critical scrutiny and systematic analysis. At the beginning of the twentieth century, elements of what we would now recognize as Social Policy were taught on social work training courses. Later a separately taught subject, called Social Administration, was developed at a number of British universities. It was only during the last half of the twentieth century that the subject changed its name to Social Policy and began to be more widely recognized.

This chapter will tell the story of social policy (with a small 's' and a small 'p') up to the point that Social Policy came of age. It is a brief history of the ideas, the events and the controversies that gave rise to Social Policy. I shall start by explaining how our ideas of citizenship have developed, since citizenship is a central concept for Social Policy. Second, I turn to the role that early social policies played in sustaining the emergence of capitalism, before turning, thirdly, to the ways in which social policies have modified capitalism. Finally, I shall examine the main ideological influences that shaped the development of social policies up until the present era, and with which Social Policy must critically contend.

From Barbarianism to Civilization?

We can tell our story in a number of different ways. Perhaps the crudest view of human history is one that considers that human beings are risen from savages; that human society has progressed from barbarianism to civilization (see Elias 1978). What is distinctive about any human society is its degree of economic, social and cultural sophistication; the nature of its 'civilization'. The transition from a world in which supposedly 'primitive' beings looked after themselves in small groups to one in which social policies are required in order that a large and complex society might sustain itself can be thought, self-evidently, to constitute a process of civilization. But civilization is a state as well as a process. We are each of us defined by the civilization in which we live and to which we belong.

We shall see in chapter 7 that the basis of racism and of intolerance towards strangers or foreigners can lie in assumptions about what it means to be civilized (e.g. Miles 1989), in the way that 'Others' may be defined as less civilized in their customs and manners than 'We'. In the event, it is quite wrong to assume that people from different, or less economically developed, civilizations are or ever were primeval or barbarian. I have already mentioned in chapter 1 the anthropological evidence used by Titmuss to suggest that pre-modern societies secured wellbeing for their members through sophisticated processes of gift exchange. The evidence from social psychology suggests that the members of economically developed societies are not necessarily any 'happier' because of the wealth they enjoy (Layard 2003; NEF 2004).

Civilization, as a concept, is closely allied to the notion of citizenship. Citizenship, in its original meaning, denoted residence in a city. As we saw in chapter 1, over two thousand years ago Aristotle addressed the question of how the patrician male elite of the Athenian city-state could achieve a good life. The essence of civilization lay in urban sophistication and self-governance. Women, children, slaves and rural people were deemed, by Aristotle at least, to be insufficiently civilized to count as citizens, but free men were expected to devise policies to secure their own wellbeing. This notion of citizenship provided a basis for 'civilized' governance in the cities of ancient Greece and Rome and in the early medieval cities of Western Europe. Centuries later the idea of citizenship began to change. Its essence came to be defined more broadly in terms of the processes of governance observed by and within a nation-state.

I shall discuss the concept of the state in chapter 6, but for now I want to explain the different traditions of citizenship that were to emerge after the so-called 'Enlightenment' of the eighteenth century. In chapter 1 I mentioned a famous Parisian revolutionary slogan, and now I shall refer to another. This was an earlier cry associated with the

French Revolution of 1789 when, in protest at their subjugation to the monarchy, the people demanded *liberté, egalité, fraternité* – or 'liberty', 'equality' and 'solidarity'. In practice, demands for individual liberty and collective solidarity are potentially in conflict with one another. 'Equality', what is more, is such a slippery concept that it has been interpreted in a variety of quite different ways. And so, two ways of thinking about citizenship have developed – one liberal, the other republican (Oliver and Heater 1994; Lister 2003) – each with different implications for the social policy-making process. The liberal tradition emphasized liberty and personal freedom: it embodied what was at the time a new individualistic ethos. The republican tradition emphasized solidarity and social cohesion: though ostensibly more inclusive, it represented something much closer to the ancient Athenian notion of citizenship. Different countries have tended to work within different traditions and to interpret them in different ways, and the relevance of this will become clear in chapter 3. The point I want to make here is that neither tradition was initially concerned about *social* equality. The liberal tradition saw equality in terms of the *constitutional* equality of the individual under the law, whereas the republican tradition saw equality in terms of equality of belonging and of *mutual obligation* (see Dean 1999).

New ideas about citizenship were not at that stage translated into social policies. The sociologist T. H. Marshall (1950) has suggested that in the 'civilized' Western world the priority in the eighteenth century was not the alleviation of social conditions, but the development of civil rights; of civil liberties, property rights and legal codes. In the nineteenth century priority was accorded to the development of political rights; of rights to vote and to political participation. It was not until the twentieth century, according to Marshall, that the development of citizenship was finally completed with the emergence of what he called 'social rights', by which he meant rights to state welfare provision: rights, for example, to social security, healthcare and education. Such rights, he claimed, would secure 'a general enrichment of the concrete substance of civilised life' (1950: 33). Marshall's account is historically imprecise and highly Anglo-centric. Citizenship rights did not necessarily develop in this orderly fashion and certainly they did not develop in the same way throughout the Western world. Nevertheless this is an account that captures the sense in which the implementation of social policies became integral to the development of modern Western citizenship: the sense in which a social dimension and questions of social equality were finally brought onto the citizenship agenda. The achievement of 'social citizenship' (see Dwyer 2004a) and questions about how to interpret that concept have played an important part in Social Policy.

The Making of Capitalism

The process by which modern forms of citizenship emerged was never a simple transition from barbarianism to civilization. It entailed all kinds of political, military and social conflicts. But it has been a process closely associated with the rise of capitalism (see Turner 1986). Capitalism, its development and its consequences (both good and bad) are central to what Social Policy has so far been about and this is another way in which to tell our story. It was the fundamental changes associated with the transition from feudalism to capitalism that gave birth to the earliest forms of social policy. And it is the subsequent dynamics of capitalism, both on a local and a global scale, that continue to shape the way that social policies develop.

The feudal social order that typified medieval European societies was characterized by the absolute rule of monarchs, by a concentration of delegated power in the hands of aristocracies and by a situation in which the vast majority of the population were serfs living, quite literally, on the land. Their lives were, by and large, (to borrow Thomas Hobbes' words) 'nasty, brutish and short' (Hobbes 1651). They eked out their existence from the land by the leave of their feudal lords, to whom they had to return a proportion of their produce. The transition to capitalism involved a number of processes:

1 The emergence of a new 'middle' class that was determined to secure for itself some of the privileges enjoyed by the aristocracy. The result, in time, was a diminution of monarchical and aristocratic power and the emergence of various forms of constitutional government that consolidated the power of what would become a capitalist class.
2 The expansion of international trade and of market systems based on concepts of property and individual ownership. The revolutionary idea was that property was not something vested by divine right in the monarchs of Europe; it ought not to be granted or seized at will. Not only should rights of ownership be personal, but all property was by nature 'alienable'; that is, it could change hands; it was something that could be bought or sold. This idea made possible contractually-based trade not only in raw materials and manufactured goods, but also in land and real estate. The power of the new capitalist class was founded on property. Such thinking also led on to the concept of wage labour: the equally revolutionary idea that

the labour power of an otherwise propertyless member of the working class was theirs to 'sell' to an employer.
3 Advances in science and technology that made possible an agrarian and then an industrial revolution, the effects of which were to force the 'common' people from the land and into wage labour. The landless poor gradually lost such traditional rights or privileges as they had had on the land and were obliged or coerced to join the agricultural labour force or to migrate towards the expanding conurbations and the new centres of manufacturing production (e.g. Hobsbawm 1962).

This thumbnail sketch neglects, amongst other things, the particular fate of peasant farmers, craft workers and the part played by many other social groups, the significance of whom varied considerably from country to country. The purpose of this narrative, however, is to illustrate how social policies necessarily developed in order to support the process of capitalist industrialization (Wilensky 1975).

Laws relating to the control of the poor had begun to develop across medieval Europe. Initially, these were contrived to control people displaced from the land by punishing vagrancy and begging, and by insisting that those who could not support themselves should not wander the country but return to the parish in which they had been born. If we take the English Poor Laws as an example, this principle continued to apply until the nineteenth century. What the Poor Laws did, as the feudal system began to unravel, was to head off wholesale social disorder; they systematized alms-giving by entrusting responsibility for relieving the poor to the local parish, which was empowered to levy a rate or tax upon local property owners to meet the cost. There could be huge variations in the degree of severity or generosity with which the poor would be treated, but the fate of the landless and the dispossessed was not left entirely to the mercy of emerging market forces.

In the course of the nineteenth century, if we continue to take England as a forerunner and example, a number of changes occurred (see, for example, Fraser 1984). First, the Poor Law was updated. Local schemes were brought under central control and a more rigorous test was introduced by which to distinguish between the deserving and the undeserving poor. The intention was that relief for the poor would only be available upon admission to a workhouse, where the conditions would be at least as harsh as those endured by the poorest self-sufficient labourer. The object was to bolster the operation of a 'free' labour market, by ensuring that all who were sane and able-bodied should work – never mind where or upon what terms such work might be found. Second, public health legislation was introduced in order to attend to the appalling insanitary conditions prevalent in overcrowded and growing conurbations. The motivation was not necessarily humanitarian. Highly contagious diseases, like cholera, could affect rich and poor alike and preventative health measures were necessary both to safeguard the health of the industrial middle class and to maximize the efficiency of industrial production. Third, towards the end of this period, factory legislation was introduced in order to limit the exploitation and reduce the risks faced by industrial workers. Once again, the motivation was not entirely humanitarian. It was recognized that this was needed in order to provide a 'level playing field' in the competition between capitalist employers, some of whom would otherwise attempt to get away with practices to which not all were prepared to stoop – and which, in any event, were likely to prove unsustainable and therefore counterproductive in the long run. Finally, legislation to provide for elementary education was introduced, not so much to benefit the working classes as to fit them to the requirements of the new economic and constitutional order.

This gloomy tale presupposes that early social policies were concerned not primarily with the promotion of human wellbeing, but with the needs of industrial capitalism.

The Taming of Capitalism

However, there is yet another story that may be told. We have already seen (in chapter 1) how Richard Titmuss hailed the twentieth-century welfare state as a way of sustaining gift-relationships. He argued that the role of social policies was partially to compensate for the 'diswelfares' occasioned by modern capitalism (Titmuss 1968). Marshall (whom we discussed above) was even more upbeat since he believed the welfare state could, without undermining the efficacy of the market system, ameliorate the class differences and conflicts associated with capitalism.

Self-evidently, in developed countries, capitalism has raised living standards for rich and poor alike. Even capitalism's fiercest critic, Karl Marx, acknowledged that capitalism was superior to feudalism, claiming that it had 'rescued a considerable portion of the population from the idiocy of rural life' (Marx and Engels 1848: 20). Certainly, the prosperity created by capitalism was to make the introduction of certain kinds of social policy possible and, in time, brought considerable benefits to the working classes. Towards the end of the nineteenth and in the course of the twentieth centuries most developed countries witnessed an expansion of social policies (see, for example, Thane 1982).

First, there were moves to modify the harsher aspects of the Poor Laws. Using the English example, it became possible for more and more categories of the 'deserving' poor to receive 'out relief' – that is, to receive relief in cash or kind without being incarcerated in the workhouse – and, in this way, contemporary forms of means-tested social assistance were born. There were moves to have vulnerable children fostered out, rather than sent to the workhouse, and to provide separate medical wings or infirmaries for those who claimed relief because of frailty or ill health. Second, across the developed world there were moves to establish social insurance systems. These entailed a form of social protection quite distinct from the Poor Law and without the Poor Law's stigmatizing effects. In return for regular contributions from a worker's wages, such schemes provided guaranteed benefits or pensions to the workers, and sometimes to members of their families, in the event of sickness, unemployment and/or upon retirement. Sometimes these schemes built upon or incorporated schemes that had been instituted by mutual or friendly societies, trade unions or other independent bodies. The cover they provided did not necessarily extend to the whole of the workforce; they did not necessarily make generous provision or provide for every kind of need or contingency; and, in any event, they did not provide for those who were not workers. Third, all developed countries eventually established compulsory state-funded education systems. Fourth, many great cities began to use local revenues not only to improve sanitation and clear their slums, but more generally to improve their municipal infrastructure through the provision of public libraries, parks and cultural facilities. Finally, many countries developed significant social housing programmes: in the British context these began after the First World War when the government promised 'homes fit for heroes' for the returning troops.

In chapter 1 I referred to what Gøsta Esping-Andersen has called the 'golden age of the welfare state', the period immediately following the Second World War when many Western countries took steps further to extend or consolidate social policy provision (see, for example, Timmins 2001). The term 'welfare state' is attributed to Archbishop William Temple and it was intended to capture the idea that the enormous power arrogated by the 'warfare state' could be applied for just as mighty, but benign, purposes in peacetime. The British case exemplified this, with the creation in the 1940s of a fully comprehensive National Insurance scheme and a National Health Service, and with significant extension of state education, housing and other forms of social welfare provision. I shall have more to say about these services and what has become of them in chapter 4, but the point to be emphasized is the supreme optimism of the period. The post-war reforms were based largely on a report by Sir

William Beveridge, a former civil servant and academic, who later became a Liberal peer. Beveridge claimed that the designs recommended in his report would vanquish the 'five giants' on the road to post-war reconstruction. The giants were Want, Disease, Ignorance, Squalor and Idleness (Beveridge 1942). This rhetorical optimism was eventually punctured in the 1970s, when a combination of factors led to the 'crisis of welfare' that I shall be discussing in chapter 9. It was, paradoxically perhaps, not just the rise but also the fall or crisis of the welfare state that gave impetus to Social Policy as an academic subject. It was at the point when optimism faltered and debate began as to whether capitalism could be tamed by social policies that Social Policy came of age.

Social Policy, as a subject, recognizes the ambiguity of capitalist social policies. One of the more extreme expressions of that ambiguity has been provided by Claus Offe who argues that 'while capitalism cannot coexist *with*, neither can it exist *without* the welfare state' (1974). Using a football (soccer) metaphor, this has been jokingly dubbed 'the Offe side trap' (Jacobs 1996). It is, however, a very apposite joke, since it captures the sense in which the mutually adopted rules of class contest can be continually exploited by one side to frustrate the other. What is more, as will become clear throughout this book, Social Policy is not only concerned with capitalist social policies. Inescapably, however, it is the social policies that were developed under capitalism that provide the historical backdrop and intellectual legacy for Social Policy.

Welfare and Ideology

The job that Social Policy has taken on is that of making sense of and moving beyond the ideological conflicts that have surrounded the development of capitalist social policies. In tracing these conflicts, we encounter a bewildering array of sometimes less than helpful labels describing different ideological variants (e.g. 'social liberalism' and 'neo-conservatism'). In the froth of party politics, parties adapt and change so that the names by which they are known bear little relation to the current ideological fashions that they are seeking either to mould or to mimic. In the real world we encounter hybrid ideologies founded on compromises and contradictions. However, like it or not, it is through political and ideological discourse that the very language of capitalist social policy has been constructed. Let me illustrate this.

So far, I have made quite sparing use of the term 'welfare' in relation to social policy provision. This is partly, as I have already said, because the word doesn't quite capture everything that is meant by my preferred

word, 'wellbeing'. But partly it is because recent ideological controversy over the nature and purpose of social policies has meant that the term has acquired a pejorative connotation. In the transition from Poor Law regimes to capitalist welfare states, the use of the word 'welfare' signalled an important change of emphasis: social policies were not just about the regulation of the poor, but the fitness of the population at large. Perversely, however, at the beginning of the twenty-first century – particularly in the US, and increasingly in the UK and elsewhere – the very word 'welfare' is associated, as the Poor Laws had been, with stigmatizing services for the poor and undeserving. This *linguistic* shift may be taken as just one piece of evidence for an underlying reversal or change of *ideological* climate.

Long before this recent change it had been possible to identify extreme positions – at opposite poles of the ideological spectrum – which rejected the very idea of a capitalist welfare state (for useful summaries see George and Wilding 1985; 1994). On the extreme right of the ideological spectrum were those who adopted a strictly economistic interpretation of liberalism, and who saw the welfare state as an unwarranted interference with free market forces and a constraint upon individual freedom. On the extreme left of the ideological spectrum, there was a crude variant of Marxism that saw the welfare state as part of a capitalist conspiracy to control the working class and prevent a socialist revolution. In between these extremes, however, there was an ideological arena not of consensus, but in which a number of different sorts of justification for capitalist social policies vied with each other. It is possible, broadly speaking, to identify four types of ideological justification and I use the diagram in figure 2.1 to illustrate these.

In figure 2.1, it may be seen immediately that I do not make a simple distinction between 'left-wing' and 'right-wing' ideologies. That just doesn't work. In fact I use two kinds of distinction. The first (which is illustrated along the horizontal axis of the diagram) is the distinction I have already made between liberal and republican conceptions of citizenship. It is important to repeat that there is often a substantial mismatch between contemporary party-political labels that may retain references to the terms 'Liberal' or 'Republican' and the original roots of those terms, which were associated with a fundamental distinction between values to do with individual freedom on the one hand and with social solidarity on the other. The second distinction (which is illustrated along the vertical axis of the diagram) is that between conservative and egalitarian ideologies. Here I am using the term 'conservative' in its most literal sense in order to distinguish between an approach that seeks to preserve the existing social order, regardless of inequalities, and one that seeks in some way to redress social inequalities. In this way, the diagram

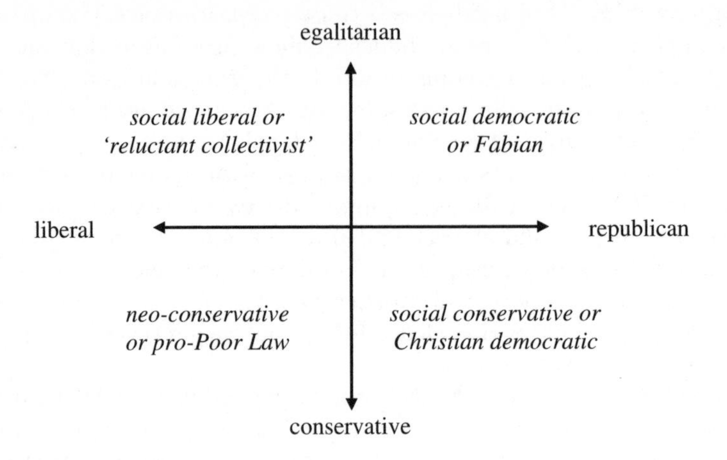

Warnings:
1. This kind of diagram is what social scientists sometimes call a 'heuristic device'. It is not meant to be an accurate depiction that accounts for every variation, but to simplify and help us understand phenomena that are especially complex or dynamic. Such diagrams, however, don't work for everyone. If it doesn't work for you, don't worry!
2. This particular diagram has evolved and is slightly different from versions I have used before – for example, in Dean 1999.

Figure 2.1 Four ideological justifications for capitalist social policies

defines four quadrants, each representing a different approach to social policy or 'welfare'.

First, we have the *egalitarian/liberal* or 'social liberal' approach. George and Wilding dubbed the egalitarian liberals the 'reluctant collectivists' (1985: ch. 3). Arguably, it was social liberalism more than any other ideology that helped to shape the world's post Second World War welfare state regimes, especially in the English-speaking world. Amongst the figures I have already mentioned it is Beveridge who stands out as a social liberal. We have seen that liberalism subscribes to an individualistic rather than a collectivist or solidaristic ethos. But social liberalism recognized that capitalism, left to its own devices, could lead to unacceptable inequalities between individuals. US President Franklin D. Roosevelt (1944) once famously declared that 'Necessitous men are not free men'. Social liberals were therefore prepared to acknowledge a specific but limited role for the state in ensuring that the theoretical equality of its citizens should not be compromised by such practical obstacles as those that Beveridge portrayed as Want, Disease, Ignorance, Squalor or Idleness. Social liberals were not out to ensure complete social equality, but to secure a national minimum for every citizen, a minimum on which each individual would be free to build for him or herself. (However, as we shall later see, the Beveridgean vision tended to assume that it would be the male breadwinner citizen who would be free to build for himself and his dependent wife and family.)

Second, (moving clockwise around the quadrants of the diagram in figure 2.1), we have what might be called the *egalitarian/republican* or what is more usually described as the 'social democratic' approach. In its purest form the welfare state is, or was, a quintessentially social democratic ideal. Social democrats are enthusiastic, not reluctant, collectivists. However, they tend towards a moderate or 'Fabian' form of socialism. The Fabian Society, founded in England in 1884, drew its name from the Roman General, Fabius Maximus, who had been known for the effective use of the tactic of delay: its aim was to achieve socialism by stealth. Social democracy, therefore, does not reject capitalism, but seeks to change it by democratic means from within; specifically, by making it more egalitarian. It is generally associated with the trade union and labour movements, though many leading twentieth-century academics, like Richard Titmuss, had more or less explicit social democratic or Fabian leanings. Social democracy has had an important influence on the development of social policies throughout the developed world, but, as we shall see in chapter 3, it is most clearly expressed in the way the Scandinavian welfare states have developed.

Third, we have the *conservative/republican* or social conservative approach. This is an approach associated with what is known as 'One Nation Toryism' in the British context, or Christian Democracy in the continental European context. In the classic republican tradition that I have mentioned above, social conservatism values social unity, not social equality. It advocates compassion for the disadvantaged, albeit within the bounds of a hierarchical social order in which decisions are brokered between society's most powerful interest groups. One of the key figures within this tradition is Otto von Bismarck who, as Germany's Chancellor between 1871 and 1890, was responsible for laying the foundations for a particular style of welfare state. Bismarck was in fact a pioneer of social insurance, but his object was thereby to weaken the influence of Germany's growing trade union movement and to use state power to underwrite certain traditional values. Social conservatism accommodates, rather than embraces, capitalism. It will sustain relatively generous social policies in order to protect but not change society.

Finally, we have the ostensibly contradictory *conservative/liberal* approach. This is not necessarily an approach that may be directly associated with any particular kind of welfare state, although it has had a certain impact on capitalist social policies. It represents, in part, what is dubbed the 'neo-conservative' approach, associated, for example, with British Prime Minister Margaret Thatcher and US President Ronald Reagan in the 1980s. But it also represents a certain 'pro-Poor Law' approach: an approach that preceded the creation of modern welfare states and which yet retains a strong influence. Thatcher and Reagan's neo-conservatism was characterized by a desire for a free economy and a strong state (Gamble 1988). It combined economic liberalism with moral authoritarianism and a desire to harness state power in order to instil moral values and shape individual behaviour. Similarly, England's classic nineteenth-century Poor Law, as we have seen, was designed to sustain free markets by regulating the behaviour of the undeserving poor. There were always those who resisted the transition from Poor Law to welfare state and it is their influence that has sought at various moments to restrain or to roll back egalitarian social policies while fostering coercive or disciplinary social policies. This is the enduring tradition that succeeds in giving 'welfare' a bad name.

The point about Social Policy as a subject is that, thankfully perhaps, it is not confined to these ideological approaches. In future chapters we shall see how, for example, feminist, anti-racist, anti-disablist, green and anti-globalization ideologies can transcend these traditional ideological conflicts. However, Social Policy cannot address new ways of thinking without an objective understanding of the foundations on which existing ways of thinking have been built. The student of Social Policy needs to be streetwise and critical.

Summary

This chapter has explained the background to Social Policy as an academic subject through the telling of four different kinds of story about the way that social policies have developed:

- First, there is the story of how human beings have progressed from simple to complex forms of society. In the process of becoming 'civilized', we have developed concepts and practices of citizenship. Citizenship as a mode of governance has been understood as having several potential elements, associated with civil liberties and political enfranchisement on the one hand, but also a social element associated with entitlements to state welfare provision.
- Second, there is the story of how capitalism succeeded feudalism. This process had to be managed by means of social policies to ensure, for example, that the displacement of people from the land was orderly; to regulate the consequences of rapid urbanization; to support the

functioning of wage labour; to regulate unfair competition between employers; to secure the standards of health and literacy required for the functioning of a capitalist democracy.

- Third, there is the story of how the welfare state was able to tame the excesses of capitalism. The development of social policies has compensated the working classes for the adverse consequences that capitalism might otherwise have had. What is more, the development of comprehensive schemes of social protection, healthcare, state education, public housing and a range of public and municipal services has allowed the working classes to reap certain advantages from capitalism.
- Finally, there is the story of ideological conflict over the nature and extent of social policies under capitalism. This was never a simple contest between 'right' and 'left', so much as the working out of uneasy compromises between, on the one hand, different interpretations of citizenship, and on the other, different approaches to the questions of equality and social order.

3

Why on Earth does it Matter?

We have seen that certain developed countries, like the UK, continue to spend quite massively on their social policies, but I suggested in chapter 2 that Social Policy as an academic subject came of age at the point when commitment to such spending seemed to be faltering. The point here is that Social Policy is about much more than picking over the runes of the past. It is about the challenges of the future and about human well-being in a worldwide context. In this chapter I shall firstly discuss the implications of the process that is generally known as 'globalization'. Second, I shall explain how social policy arrangements appear currently to be functioning – or not functioning – in different parts of the world. Third, I shall discuss what Social Policy has to contribute to debates about the environment and the survival of our planet. Finally, I shall address recent developments in relation to social policies at the international level.

The Threat of Globalization?

Globalization is a contested concept. That is to say, there are disagreements as to what the term means or whether, as a phenomenon, it really exists at all. Sometimes these disagreements are discussed in terms of a 'strong' versus a 'weak' globalization thesis (see Yeates 2001).

The 'strong' thesis argues that in the twenty-first century global capitalism has been emancipated from political control; that the nation state and its power to pursue social policies are now things of the past;

that economic liberalism now reigns supreme. Such claims represent a simplified account of some rather complex phenomena. We may see that trade has become increasingly international; finance capital has become increasingly mobile and will invest wherever in the world it can make the quickest profit; the huge transnational corporations that are now emerging have more power and wealth than many individual nation states; manufacturing processes have become more flexible and are rapidly relocatable; new information and communication technologies have speeded up the world and fundamentally changed the nature of the global economy; organized labour has been weakened and low or unskilled workers suffer enforced immobility and low wages; the poorer countries of the world are denied fair access to global markets and face systemic obstacles to economic development.

In addition to these economic processes, there have been worldwide political and cultural changes. Old communist or state-socialist regimes have dissolved and commentators like Francis Fukuyama (1992) claim that, with the final ideological triumph of capitalism, we have seen the end of history as we knew it. Rapid transport links and pervasive communication media make the world effectively smaller, and some claim that systems of governance and processes of management tend to conform to increasingly similar assumptions (Meyer et al. 1997), others that we are witnessing the 'McDonaldization' (Ritzer 2004) or 'Disneyfication' (Fevre 2000) of cultural life as people around the world not only organize themselves in similar ways but aspire to eat, dress and entertain themselves according to increasingly similar norms.

The 'weak' thesis would say that these claims are over-inflated. It acknowledges that recent decades have seen increased global flows of capital, people, information and ideas and these are associated with changes, for example, in the way that local labour markets function; that there are certain characteristic fiscal and demographic pressures that the developed nations seem to have in common; and correspondingly there are problems that must be addressed if the poorest countries are to compete with their richer neighbours. It is acknowledged that there is a risk of a 'race to the bottom' between nation states as they compete to lower social standards in order to attract internal investment. But, on the other hand, it is argued that regional and international forums and organizations have a role to play and are of growing importance to processes of governance around the world; it appears that capitalism still needs social policy interventions since even all-powerful transnational corporations need local stability in order to function on the ground; that social policies can be used to enhance national competitiveness and may actually help national economies to integrate themselves into the wider global economy (Gough 2000; Leibfried 2000).

Insofar as claims about globalization capture something of what is going on, there are several different ways of thinking about the implications. With tongue somewhat in cheek, Tony Fitzpatrick (2001: pp. 164–5) has attempted to herd the multiplicity of commentators on the subject into four main camps:

The Sponsors' camp. Commentators like Fukuyama (see above) embrace the idea of globalization as a cause. According to the Sponsors, human wellbeing will be served by global market forces and not by national governments.

The Sceptics' camp. Followers of the political Third Way (Giddens 1998; 2001) acknowledge there are major changes afoot, but insist that national governments can still make a difference. However, the role of a government, according to the Sceptics, is to promote the international competitiveness of their national labour forces and to provide the framework within which responsible citizens will provide, so far as possible, for their own wellbeing.

The Doubters' camp. There are commentators who claim there is nothing new afoot. Globalization and the internationalization of trade – as we observed in chapter 2 – have been going on for centuries and, in any event, there are still many spheres of economic activity that have not been, and are unlikely to become, global in nature (Hirst and Thompson 1996). National interests still prevail in social policy matters and, according to the Doubters, social protectionism and the welfare state will survive.

The Hecklers' camp. The emerging anti-globalization movement represents a complex alliance of disparate factions that challenge the global ascendancy of capitalism, liberal democracy, Western culture and neo-liberal welfare theories. It burst upon the world in Seattle in 1999 with the first of many violent demonstrations in opposition to the World Trade Organization summits, and it moved on in Porto Alegre in 2001 to establish the first in a series of vibrant annual debates under the banner of the World Social Forum. Its more radical elements reject the possibility that human wellbeing can be assured under global capitalism and advocate unconditional resistance. But there are those within its ranks (see Callinicos 2003) that argue for transitional strategies, based on an anti-capitalist agenda.

I shall return to discuss some of these alternative strategies in greater detail in chapter 10. For now, however, we need to row back from thinking about future prospects and to try and make sense of the different ways in which social policies are being organized at present.

Welfare Regimes

Social Policy does this by using theories that distinguish different kinds of welfare 'regime'. Although it was not the only or even the first such attempt, one of the most influential schemes or models for the classification of social policy arrangements or regimes has been that provided by the Danish theorist, Gøsta Esping-Andersen (1990). Esping-Andersen used statistical indicators to distinguish between the performances of different capitalist welfare states and he argued from the results that – towards the end of the twentieth century – countries could be grouped together into three main types:

'Liberal' welfare regimes. These, by and large, are English-speaking countries – such as the USA, Canada and, increasingly, the UK and Ireland – that have *relatively* modest levels of public spending on social policies, where welfare benefits tend to be means-tested, and where public services may be selectively provided. These regimes tend to encourage occupational fringe benefits and private or market-led forms of welfare provision. We are dealing here in generalizations and, prior to the 1970s, for example, the UK would probably not have been classified as a liberal regime (and even now, its universal National Health Service makes it untypical among liberal regimes). The term 'liberal' in Esping-Andersen's model identifies the *anti*-collectivist influence of classical, economic or 'neo'-liberalism, though in practice liberal welfare regimes reflect in differing degrees the *reluctant* collectivist influence of social liberalism that we have already identified in chapter 2 above (in the top left-hand quadrant of figure 2.1).

'Conservative' welfare regimes. These, by and large, are Western continental European countries – such as Germany and France – that have higher levels of public spending on social policies, where welfare benefits tend to be social insurance based, but where particular importance is placed on the role of families as opposed to public services. These regimes are strongly 'corporatist': that is, there is an emphasis on policy negotiation between the principal 'social partners', namely, capital (business interests), labour (workers' interests) and the state (government interests). The term 'conservative' signals the influence of the kind of social conservatism that we identified in chapter 2 (in the bottom right-hand quadrant of figure 2.1).

'Social Democratic' welfare regimes. These, by and large, are Scandinavian countries – such as Sweden and Denmark – that have the highest levels of public spending on social policies, where welfare benefits and public services tend to be generous and, in practice, almost universal

> in their coverage. Such regimes have sometimes been described as 'socialist', but the term 'social democratic' is more apposite and reflects the influence of the kind of social democracy that we identified in chapter 2 (in the top right-hand quadrant of figure 2.1). It is important to emphasize that such regimes are still capitalist and place considerable emphasis on achieving full employment and high productivity.

Esping-Andersen's model has been criticized on a number of fronts. First, it has been roundly condemned by feminists, because the differences on which the model focuses relate primarily to the experiences of men, rather than women. Differences between welfare states can also be analysed in terms of the extent to which they benefit women and, specifically, to which they enable women by giving them freedom to enter the labour market and freedom from patriarchal control within the family (e.g. Lewis 1992). I shall discuss this further in chapter 7.

Second, the model can be criticized because there are some countries for which it cannot adequately account. Most countries in practice are hybrids: that is, they combine the features of more than one model. Additionally, some welfare regimes exhibit the effects of other influences, including – in recent welfare reforms in the USA, for example – a moral authoritarianism consistent with the sort of neo-conservatism that we identified in chapter 2 (in the bottom left-hand quadrant of figure 2.1). Esping-Andersen himself insists that it is always possible to identify a dominant influence (Esping-Andersen 1999). It may be argued, for example, that Australia and New Zealand are unique, because, despite their heavy reliance on means-testing, they are more generous than other liberal regimes; but Esping-Andersen claims they are still essentially liberal. It may be argued that the Netherlands has strongly social democratic as well as conservative features; that Japan has a distinctive mixture of liberal and conservative features; and that the southern European countries – Spain, Italy and Greece – are emerging as an altogether different kind of welfare regime; but Esping-Andersen claims that all these countries are essentially conservative. There is always room for argument. However, beyond the accepted boundaries of the capitalist world there are places where models like that of Esping-Andersen don't necessarily work: in post-communist or 'transition' countries, and in developing or 'Third World' countries.

Turning first to the post-communist countries, prior to the collapse in 1989 of the Soviet Union and its satellite states across Central and Eastern Europe, the Soviet world exhibited its own distinctive welfare regime based on guaranteed employment, subsidized prices and extensive state-enterprise-based social benefits. The level of wages, benefits and pensions was low and the standard of health and housing provision, for all but the Communist Party elite, was often poor. None the less, when this was swept away in a headlong pursuit of free market reforms, the result was a cataclysmic increase in poverty and inequality, from which many individual countries, including Russia, are still struggling to recover. Some of the more economically successful countries, such as the Czech Republic, Hungary and Poland, which have now joined the European Union, have adapted or reconstructed their welfare infrastructure in ways that accommodate certain of the liberal principles espoused by the world's international financial institutions (which we shall discuss below). However, the outcome, according to Bob Deacon (1997), is in some respects more akin to social liberalism than neo-liberalism. The remaining countries, however, appear to be developing in the direction of what Deacon has called 'post-communist conservative corporatism'. The three characteristically most powerful social groups within these countries – the new super-rich capitalist elite, the Communist 'old guard' and organized elements of the working class – are increasingly willing to accede to pragmatic policy compromises by which unrestrained economic growth may be sacrificed in order to achieve modest levels of social protection. Unfortunately, such attempts are being undermined by the massive scale of unregulated and illegal economic activities.

Turning, finally, to the world's 'developing' countries – a term that is widely used to denote those nations that are not members of the Organization for Economic Co-operation and Development (OECD) – the point to be grasped is that the fundamental assumptions that inform the classification of capitalist welfare state regimes do not necessarily apply. The norms of a functioning labour market and the writ of a legitimate state apparatus do not necessarily run throughout such countries. Ian Gough, Geoff Wood and colleagues (2004) have recently suggested an alternative form of classification scheme that distinguishes between:

The welfare state regimes that are emergent, for example, in several Latin American countries. These countries have developing capitalist economies and a specific colonial heritage that once favoured unevenly developed conservative welfare regimes. But under the tutelage of international financial institutions they are beginning to adopt policies more characteristic of liberal welfare regimes, albeit that – just as in some of the post-communist countries – these regimes are having to co-exist with an extensive unregulated or informal economy.

The productivist regimes typical of East Asia. The so-called 'tiger economies' of East Asia are, once again, clearly capitalist in nature. While some have argued that, like Japan, these regimes are informed by traditional Confucian values that make them conservative in nature, Gough and Wood point to the distinctive way in which these regimes prioritize economic production over social policy.

The informal security regimes typical of South Asia. The colonial heritage of the South Asian sub-continent has left countries in some instances with quite cumbersome state bureaucracies, but often dysfunctional economies. Practical provision for human wellbeing still depends heavily on informal mechanisms: on family, kinship and local community.

The insecurity regimes characteristic of many countries in sub-Saharan Africa. Such welfare entitlements as exist in such countries do so in the face of an anarchic competition for survival. They depend on such protection as is offered by local leaders, warlords, chieftains, mafia bosses, corrupt officials and benign aid workers.

This still leaves several parts of the world unclassified and unaccounted for. In particular, the Middle Eastern/North African region, that includes several semi-feudal oil-rich states; and China, which is the most populous nation on earth and the last major communist nation to survive. Social Policy is only just beginning to study and to understand these (see, for example, Finer-Jones 2003).

Regime theory does not provide all the answers. It is only a tool. However, it is a tool that helps us – to analyse how the world is changing; to see to what extent, in response to the pressures of globalization, different approaches to promoting human wellbeing may be converging; alternatively, to understand how, despite such pressures, some countries may be 'path dependent' and unable to change.

Ecology and Human Welfare

In discussing the wellbeing of the human species there is an overriding consideration to which we must now turn. Is life on earth sustainable? It is an issue for Social Policy as much as for the natural sciences. Social policies of the past have addressed certain environmental issues through public health legislation and urban planning, but Social Policy as an academic subject was born at or about the same time as the Green movement. The Green movement was about more than the environment; it was, and is, about ecology. It was in the 1970s that a scientific case began to emerge in support of the argument that there are limits to economic growth and consumption (Meadows et al. 1972). It isn't simply that industrial capitalism was polluting the planet, something that could possibly be fixed, but that by its activities an ever more numerous and invasive human species was depleting the natural resources of the earth and systematically degrading it. A more mystical claim – the Gaia hypothesis (Lovelock 1979) – held that the earth itself is a self-sustaining living organism and will in time heal itself by eliminating the species that has infected it and which is threatening its future survival. If the human species does not destroy itself by its own military Armageddon, it will be destroyed by an ecological Armageddon. If such beliefs were regarded as eccentric in the 1970s, there was more palpable cause for alarm during the 1980s. In 1986 the Chernobyl nuclear reactor, in what is now the Ukraine, exploded, causing radioactive contamination on an international scale, an incident that emphasized to the world not only the hazards associated with human technologies, but also their global consequences. At the same time the evidence was mounting that carbon dioxide and other emissions from human activity were creating a 'greenhouse' effect that would lead to global warming and, ultimately, catastrophic climate change.

In response a United Nations Commission laid out proposals for how we might yet achieve 'sustainable development' (Brundtland 1987). It was contended not that there is some absolute limit to the amount of economic growth the planet can sustain, but that 'technology and social organization can be both managed and improved to make way for a new era in economic growth' (ibid: 8). The object was to ensure that present generations should meet their needs in ways that will not compromise the ability of future generations to do so, and in ways that will ensure the poorer nations of the world do not miss out on the benefits of economic growth. Subsequent United Nations summits have established agreements that were supposed, for example, to commit member nations to the principles of sustainable development (the Rio summit of 1992) and to a protocol to limit carbon emissions and restrict climate change (the Kyoto summit of 1997). However, compliance with such agreements has generally been dismal (see, for example, Cahill 2002).

Social Policy has sought to engage with ecological perspectives (for example, George and Wilding 1994: ch. 7; Fitzpatrick 1998) but not necessarily as vigorously as it should. The growth of capitalist social policies and the emergence of the welfare state were part and parcel of the industrialization process and were a consequence of economic growth. The welfare state is implicated in the development of unsustainable industrial societies. The challenge for Social Policy is to envisage how to attend to the promotion of human wellbeing in ways that do not involve the harnessing of economic growth. In chapter 2, I discussed the different ways in which capitalist social policies could be ideologically justified. It is possible in a quite similar way to characterize four different ways of thinking about social policies from an ecological perspective (see Dean 2001):

Ecological modernization. This is what is sometimes referred to as a 'light green' or environmentalist approach (to distinguish it from the 'deep ecology' approach that I shall discuss below). Amongst those in the world who take the threat of ecological disaster seriously, this is probably the dominant view (see, for example, Dryzek 1997). However, it is not necessarily a view that engages directly with Social Policy, since it is concerned primarily with economic not social imperatives. It is the ecological modernizers who believe in sustainable development. They believe the ecological problem can be managed without impairing economic growth; that there is, or will be, a technological fix for every environmental hazard; that there should even be an economic payback from the development of new environmentally friendly technologies. The emphasis, therefore, is on clean production techniques, renewable energy sources and waste recycling. It is an essentially liberal approach that stresses individual responsibility and may, for example, favour the use of tax incentives in order to encourage companies and people to adopt new non-polluting technologies or to adapt to low-energy consumption lifestyles. The underlying assumption is that the consolidation or development of social policies that depend on economic growth will be allowed to continue.

Eco-socialism. The essence of the eco-socialist approach is the idea of a 'non-productivist design' for social policies (Offe 1992). The aim is that humanity should realize its full social potential within its ecological context. It is capitalism not humanity that threatens the earth. The emancipation of human beings from capitalist exploitation is the necessary condition for the emancipation of the earth itself (Bookchin 1991). While radical proponents of eco-socialism would aim to roll back capitalism, its more moderate supporters address the possibility that we might limit economic production so as to produce no more than is necessary to meet human needs; and that we should redistribute income and resources – at both a local and a global level – so that everybody's needs are satisfied. In practical terms this might entail a universal reduction of working hours, giving people more time for caring responsibilities and for leisure. In particular, it would suggest the introduction of basic income (or citizen's income) schemes. The idea of a basic income has attracted support for different reasons from across the political spectrum, but its eco-socialist proponents seek to develop it as a form of universal social dividend sufficient to meet the basic needs of every man, woman and child. I shall return to this idea in chapter 10, but the point for now is that eco-socialist social policies would seek to guarantee human wellbeing despite reductions in economic production. The object is sustainable social justice.

Green communitarianism. This is a term that captures a spectrum of ideas that celebrate the place of the human species in nature, but which is not necessarily concerned with social justice. The emphasis is on the natural, rather than the social. It is within this approach that the idea that we should protect the environment for the benefit of future generations holds particular sway. There are questions here not only about the sacrifices that present generations should be prepared to make, but also about how future generations are to be prepared – in terms of their skills and priorities – for life on earth. It is an essentially conservative approach that questions the wisdom of scientific and technological progress and seeks to defend the existing order against the 'manufactured risks' (Beck 1992) of the contemporary era. At one extreme, it can favour rather romantic or spiritual notions about 'oneness with Nature'; about traditions of self-sufficiency and communal governance. At the other, it can sustain potentially innovative ideas and social practices, such as the development of local economic trading schemes (or LETS) – informal neighbourhood-based arrangements by which members of a community realize the scope of their skills and capacities through an organized exchange of mutual services. Certain elements of green communitarianism are evident, for example, in discussions about the ways in which sustainable urban communities can be developed and managed (Rogers and Power 2000).

Deep ecology. The three approaches described above are all anthropocentric: that is, they place human interests first. Deep ecology places the interests of the earth first – above those of humanity (Fox 1984). At best, it places the human species on a par with other species and favours, for example, enforced reductions in living standards and, if necessary, coercive steps to limit human population growth. At worst, it is fundamentally misanthropic and will condone punitive, even lethal, forms of direct action against human beings. Deep ecology favours policies that atone for the past excesses of the human species, but in its hostility to humanity it can also come close to eugenicist and even fascist thinking. Deep green thinking can pose a challenge to Social Policy and its concern with human wellbeing.

In practice, ecological perspectives in Social Policy draw upon a variety of ideas. We are forced to think in various ways about how major technological and lifestyle transitions, or dramatic reductions in economic growth, or significant changes in the inter-generational demands and expectations could impact on our lives. In particular, we face questions about what the implications might be for the distribution of resources in an international or global context.

Global Social Policy

This opens the door onto a debate about whether there is, or will ever be, such a thing as Global Social Policy. Bob Deacon has suggested that environmental awareness and, in particular, the realization that environmental threats are transnational in nature is one of three key factors that have led to what he calls 'the globalization of social policy and the socialization of global politics' (1997: 4). The other two factors to which he refers are, on the one hand, the end of the 'Cold War' and the collapse of Communism (already mentioned above) and, on the other, the threat of global migration stemming from the chronic political instability and economic deprivation that are experienced in various parts of the world. It is in the interests of global capitalism, according to Deacon, to try and defend the welfare states of the Northern and Western hemispheres; to export the welfare capitalist model to the Southern and Eastern hemispheres; and to achieve at least some measure of transnational redistribution in order to sustain global stability.

At the end of the twentieth century it certainly appeared that foreign policy preoccupations around the world were, for the most part, moving away from military and security matters and towards trade and economic matters. What is more, there were signs that questions to do with social and environmental matters were beginning to creep onto the agenda. More recent events – the terrorist attack on New York and Washington on 11 September 2001 and the subsequent US-led invasions of Afghanistan and Iraq – may mean that such optimism was premature. Nevertheless, the network of international governmental organizations that has developed – mainly since the Second World War (see table 3.1) – may be able in the twenty-first century to address social policy issues in a way that simply was not possible before. It has been observed, for example, that in the past 'the rhetoric of human rights was reduced to a weapon in the propaganda for geopolitical interests' (UNDP 2000: 3). But now the language of human rights can and is being used by international governmental organizations to frame global strategies to combat poverty (see, for example, OHCHR 2002). The United Nations has recently declared ambitious goals for the eradication of poverty and the promotion of human development into the twenty-first century, though

Table 3.1 Principal international governmental organizations

Types	Names	Functions
International financial institutions	International Monetary Fund (IMF)	Ensuring monetary stability/ providing credit facilities to nations in economic difficulty
	World Bank	Financing social and economic development programmes and projects
United Nations (UN)	World Health Organization (WHO) International Labour Organization (ILO) UN Development Programme (UNDP) UN High Commissioner for Human Rights (UNHCHR) UN High Commissioner for Refugees (UNHCR) UN Children's Fund (UNICEF) UN Educational, Scientific and Cultural Organization (UNESCO)	Promoting and overseeing: human rights; world peace; social and economic development
	World Trade Organization (WTO)	Regulation of world trade systems
Policy forums or 'clubs'	Organization for Economic Co-operation and Development (OECD)	Economic co-operation and development in 29 'developed' nations
	G8	Co-ordination between the 8 richest nations
	G77	Co-ordination between 77 'developing nations'

it is acknowledged that the goals present 'daunting challenges' (UNDP 2003: 13).

In addition to international governmental organizations there is, as we shall see in chapter 6, a plethora of regional governmental organizations with an increasingly important role in the shaping of social policies. At the same time, there has been a proliferation of international non-governmental organizations (NGOs), such as Oxfam, Save the Children and Médecins Sans Frontières. These, as we shall see in chapter 9, not only provide funds and services to relieve human poverty and suffering around the world, but have a significant role as policy advocates. To an extent, therefore, there are 'bottom up' influences operating within and upon the globalization process (Yeates 2001), influences capable of contributing to a global Social Policy debate.

Some, however, would argue that grounds for optimism are limited. The consensus that appears currently to inform the international governmental organizations from the 'top down' is one that favours global capitalism. It is widely described by writers such as Guy Standing (2002) as the 'Washington Consensus'. The essential elements of the consensus favours the liberalization of trade and financial markets, the privatization and deregulation of economic production, flexible labour markets, low public spending and taxation and selective social 'safety nets' (that is to say, means-tested forms of social assistance for the poorest). This, in essence, was the prescription that provided the basis of the 'structural adjustment' programmes that signally failed to alleviate poverty in many developing countries in the 1980s and that, when applied as 'shock therapy' in post-communist countries in the 1990s, had quite devastating consequences. Recent publications from the World Bank would seem on the face of things to indicate that international financial institutions might have come to recognize the limitations of the Washington Consensus (World Bank 2001), but their prescriptions for 'pro-poor governance' still emphasize public spending restraint and the use of 'safety nets'. At the same time the WTO has been attempting to broker a Multilateral Agreement on Investment that would ensure that health and social services provided under governmental authority will no longer be exempt from free trade and competition rules. Taking the stance of the World Bank and the WTO together, the implicit policy is that there should be minimal means-tested social provision for the poor, but that it should be possible for the affluent middle classes of the world to purchase human services on a competitive basis in a global market place. Commentators like Deacon and Standing – and many others – fear this will lead to two-tier welfare provision and to social inequity.

Currently, therefore, global social policy in the twenty-first century seems to be subject to some of the same influences as capitalist social policy in the twentieth century and, in particular, to the assumptions that in the late twentieth century informed so-called 'liberal' welfare state regimes. The questions for Social Policy are – what are the implications and how might change come about?

Summary

This chapter has sought to place Social Policy in its global context.

- The process known as 'globalization' has significant consequences in terms of the constraints that it appears to place on social policy provision in the developed world and the potential threats that it poses to human wellbeing in the developing world. From a Social Policy perspective there is a range of questions about what this might mean. Does it mean the end of the welfare state as we knew it? If so, would this matter? What might appear in place of the welfare state? Can globalization be resisted?
- To help answer these questions Social Policy uses theoretical models to distinguish the different kinds of social policy arrangements or 'welfare regimes' that are to be found around the world at present. It has been possible since the late twentieth century to identify three main types of capitalist welfare regime – liberal, conservative and social democratic – but these distinctions do not necessarily work for post-communist and developing countries. Insofar as post-communist countries have been able to achieve stability, it seems they may begin to approximate to capitalist welfare regimes. But there are parts of the developing world where social policies are wholly subordinate, ineffectual or non-existent.
- An overriding concern for Social Policy is the survival of the planet on which the human species lives. Awareness of the ecological hazards associated with human activities and, in particular, with global capitalism, poses critical problems for the future wellbeing of the species. Policy makers would seem, by and large, to be pursuing the goal of 'sustainable development'. It is assumed that it will be possible to maintain economic growth in ways that do not damage the environment or deplete the earth of its natural resources. Alternative approaches, however, might entail adapting constructively to the consequences of reduced economic production; reverting to more traditional or 'natural' ways of life; or, some would argue, imposing radical restrictions upon human activity.
- The possibility of environmental catastrophe, the potential consequences of a changing geopolitical order and the risks associated with

social instability and extreme poverty in various parts of the world have given impetus to the efforts of the world's international governmental organizations. On the one hand, there are signs of a transnational commitment to combating world poverty. On the other, however, the logic that seems to drive the community of international organizations implies a very particular social policy approach that some would regard as restrictive, if not unjust.

4

What does Human Wellbeing Entail?

It was explained in chapter 1 that, so far as Social Policy is concerned, the question of what human wellbeing entails is a practical, as much as a philosophical, question. Social Policy textbooks quite often focus on five key areas of social policy or human service provision: health, education, social security, housing and the personal social services. Generally, employment policy and aspects of environmental policy are also seen as key areas. However, as we shall see in chapter 9, there is a clear sense within Social Policy that any understanding of what promotes human wellbeing must also encompass a variety of factors reaching beyond the boundaries of service administration.

In this chapter, I shall nevertheless offer an extremely brief and sweeping survey of the main areas of human service provision and the corresponding institutions or systems that may characteristically go to make up a welfare state. Any one of these areas is, potentially, a specialist field of interest in its own right and students of Social Policy will usually choose at least one of these areas as a topic for in-depth study. All that this chapter will do is signal some of the distinctive issues of relevance within each area. For this limited purpose I have grouped the areas of service provision into four; first, what are often regarded as 'bedrock' human services in health and education; second, services concerned with income maintenance and employment, by which we ensure social security and economic productivity; third, services concerned with housing and the environment, by which we secure the physical contexts in which human beings live out their lives; and finally, the so-called 'personal' social services reserved for the care or protection of the most vulnerable members of society.

Health and Education

To employ the Bunyanesque metaphors popularized by Beveridge (see Timmins 2001 and chapter 2 above), specialist health and education services are required in order to tackle the giants 'Disease' and 'Ignorance'. In the course of the twentieth century the developed countries of the world – through public health and healthcare provision – have taken considerable strides in reducing the incidence of certain illnesses, in the treatment of disease and in increasing life expectancy (see Allsop 2003; Baggott 1998). They have also made progress in achieving relatively high levels of literacy within their populations and in developing the skills that workers require in an industrial economy (see David 2003; Chitty 2004).

However, Disease and Ignorance continue to stalk even the richest nations of the world. The economically developed countries have experienced what is sometimes called 'an epidemiological transition'. Instead of the kind of contagious diseases that can shorten human life, they now face the problem of the degenerative illnesses that come from living longer. They also face the health hazards associated with industrialization (such as pollution-related illness and traffic accident injuries) and with consumerism (such as smoking-related diseases and obesity). At the same time, having constructed their education systems to supply the needs of an economy dominated by manufacturing (which requires a small professional elite, modest numbers of skilled operatives and large numbers of complaisant routine workers), developed countries are currently struggling with the consequences of globalization (see chapter 3 above). In particular they must now confront the 'skills gaps' characteristically generated by the 'post-Fordist' information and service economy (e.g. Murray 1989). This kind of economy requires a significant core of highly skilled workers, in need of continual retraining, and a substantial 'flexible' periphery, capable of shifting continuously between relatively low-skilled jobs.

Sound health and at least basic literacy are widely regarded as fundamental requirements both for economic productivity and for any kind of individual quality of life. In chapter 1 we encountered the argument by Doyal and Gough (1991) that human beings' most basic needs are for personal health and critical autonomy: the first requires public infrastructure and healthcare services and the second, education. The United Nations' Millennium Development Goals include the targets set out in box 4.1.

In one sense these are quite modest goals: they do not guarantee clean water and sanitation for all; by prioritizing the health of children and

Box 4.1 Millennium Development Goals and targets relating to health and education

Goal: Ensure environmental sustainability
Target: 'Halve by 2015 the proportion of people without access to safe drinking water.'

Goal: Reduce child mortality
Target: 'Reduce by two thirds, between 1990 and 2015, the under-five mortality rate.'

Goal: Improve maternal health
Target: 'Reduce by three quarters, between 1990 and 2015, the maternal mortality ratio.'

Goal: Combat HIV/AIDS, malaria and other diseases
Targets: 'Have halted by 2015 and begun to reverse the spread of HIV/AIDS.'
'Have halted by 2015 and begun to reverse the incidence of malaria and other major diseases.'

Goal: Achieve universal primary education:
Target: 'Ensure that, by 2015, children everywhere, boys and girls alike, will be able to complete a full course of primary schooling.'

Goal: Promote gender equality and empower women:
Target: 'Eliminate gender disparity in primary and secondary education, preferably by 2005 and in all levels of education no later that 2015.'

Source: www.un.org/millenniumgoals and see UNDP 2003.

mothers they neglect the needs of, for example, older people, disabled people and people with mental health difficulties; by prioritizing primary education they neglect the need for secondary and higher education in the developing world. However, in view of the difficulties faced by some of the poorest developing countries, these are in fact ambitious goals. It is highly significant that recognition has been afforded to the risk posed by the AIDS pandemic, to the failure to eradicate infectious diseases in the developing world and to the need to prioritize considerations of gender equality. Unfortunately, there are grounds for doubting that the goals will be met.

If health and education are central concerns at the global level, they are also significant in terms of the popular support that exists for public provision in these areas. Turning our attention back to the developed world, in the UK, for example, social attitude surveys consistently show that spending on the National Health Service (NHS) and on state education is regarded as a higher priority than spending on any other aspect of the welfare state (e.g. Lipsey 1994). Everybody at some stage in their life is likely to need and make use of healthcare and education. But it is not essential that such services should be provided by the state. We saw in chapter 2 that in the past such things have not always been provided as public services and we shall see in chapter 9 that many people use various forms of 'private' healthcare and education. It may be that, in the future, those who can afford to do so will pay for their own health and education services and, within the developed world, there are countries where most people already do and have always done so. In the USA, which is the richest nation on earth, they spend more per head of population on healthcare than in the UK, but a much smaller proportion of that spending is public spending (OECD 2004). Even amongst the countries that have predominantly public healthcare and education systems, different mechanisms can be used to finance it. In the UK, the NHS is funded principally through general taxation, but in most Western continental European countries it is funded by means of social insurance. Most developed countries provide universal state-funded education at primary and secondary level (from which some parents may, if they choose, opt out), but arrangements for the funding of higher education vary considerably.

In addition to questions about how we organize payment for health and education (to which I shall return in chapter 5), policy considerations remain central to the question of who benefits. In the sphere of health, the question for policy makers is whether the primary object is to ensure national efficiency or whether it is to respond to patients' needs and interests. In the UK, for example, the National Health Insurance scheme introduced in 1911 would only cover the costs of a worker's medical treatment, and not that required for members of his or her family: the priority was to get sick workers back to work. The NHS, introduced in 1948, guaranteed all citizens access to medical treatment and subsequent reforms have increasingly given patients an element of choice as to where and by whom they are treated. But patients have never effectively been able to choose the nature and extent of their treatment.

The mechanisms by which treatments are rationed have evolved over time, but publicly provided services are bound to reflect policy priorities. This is partly because certain treatment alternatives are more expensive than others, but it also reflects ethical controversies. For example, should public funds be used to provide non-essential treatments, such as cosmetic surgery or fertility treatment? Should they be used to fund controversial procedures, such as abortion, genetic screening, or assisted euthanasia? Are some patients more deserving of treatment than others? This last question is often considered in relation to the provision of treatment for illnesses that are directly caused by unhealthy lifestyles. But, more importantly, it could also relate to whether priority should be given, on the one hand, to people who are younger, cleverer, or more useful to society, or, on the other, to those who are poorer, sicker and most disadvantaged. A major concern for Social Policy has been the extent to which, even in developed countries with sophisticated health services, there are stark and enduring variations between the health of the richest and the poorest socio-economic classes, and in the extent to which better-off and middle-class people obtain more benefit from services than poorer people (Wilkinson 1996).

Similarly, in the sphere of education there are questions as to whether provision is primarily for the benefit of society, the economy, or individual pupils. In practice, as Paul Daniel and John Ivatts (1998: 168) point out, 'rather than children's needs being placed at the forefront of education policy considerations, a variety of adult concerns and perspectives determine the policy outcomes'. Education had once been the preserve of the privileged (and, particularly, the sons of the privileged), but in the developed world it has become compulsory for all children. Taking the UK as our example, the education system developed in the post-Second World War period was explicitly intended to provide different sorts of education to suit pupils for different kinds of station in life, according to their perceived aptitudes and abilities (and, in some respects, their sex). There was a move in the 1960s towards a more comprehensive, child-centred approach to education, but the late 1970s witnessed the emergence of a 'new vocationalism' that has continued to inform education policy and has been a critical factor in the move towards a national schools' curriculum. This has been attacked by one critic as 'a battery farm model of education, in which each child, like a battery hen, is to assimilate as much as possible of the food offered to it' (Kelly 1994: 94). None the less, there is considerable evidence that poor educational attainment in childhood is a 'powerful precursor' (Hobcraft 2002: 77) to adverse adult outcomes, such as poverty. Education makes a difference. But as with health, the problem is that educational outcomes tend in the developed countries to be persistently related to socio-economic class. Children from better-off and middle-class parental backgrounds benefit more from education provision than children from poorer backgrounds (Sparkes and Glennerster 2002).

While everyone can agree that health and education services are critical for human wellbeing, Social Policy is concerned with how best to make such services work.

Income Maintenance and Employment

Going back to Beveridge's metaphorical giants, income maintenance and employment services exist to combat 'Want' and 'Idleness'. People living in a cash economy require income to sustain themselves, together with any dependent members of their household. The assumption in a capitalist society is that such income should come for the most part from paid employment. Governments may be involved through macro-economic policy in seeking to ensure full employment, and through employment legislation in regulating the terms and conditions on which people can earn income through wages. Where people cannot sustain themselves through wages (or the occupational benefits, or 'perks', provided by employers), their income may come from cash allowances, benefits or pensions. These, if they are not directly organized and paid by governments, may be subject to state regulation. Additionally, governments can in some circumstances help sustain individual incomes through fiscal benefits or tax allowances.

It is immediately apparent that this kind of provision is different in kind to health or education services. We saw in chapter 1 that, in the UK, income maintenance provision – or 'social security' as it is generically described – can account for a huge proportion of what is spent by the government, and that this is not untypical of capitalist welfare states. But this is not the same as spending on hospitals or schools. What is involved is the redistribution or transfer of cash through the tax or national insurance system. This 'transfer spending' goes into the pockets of claimants who, when they spend it to meet their subsistence needs, put the money back – just as wage earners do – into the national economy. It has been argued, controversially, that this should not be regarded as spending at all, since an affluent society can afford as much cash redistribution through taxes or contributions as it chooses (see Esam et al. 1985). Employment policy, what is more, need of itself cost nothing at all if what it entails is the manipulation of macro-economic framework and the regulation of employers. In practice there can be significant costs associated with such intervention, but more importantly – as we shall see – social security spending and the terms on which it is managed can itself be an instrument of employment policy. Social security and employment policies are closely intertwined.

What Beveridge called 'Want' is more usually referred to as poverty. Poverty is an essential concept in Social Policy. There is not space in this book to discuss all the different ways in which it may be defined and measured. However, there are two important things to grasp about poverty. The first is that it is a massive and enduring global problem. At the turn of the current millennium, of the world's 6.1 billion people, 2.8 billion (46 per cent) were living on less than US$2 per day and 1.2 billion (20 per cent) were living in 'extreme poverty', on less than US$1 per day (Townsend and Gordon 2002; UNDP 2003). The second thing to grasp is that the nature of poverty in the developed world has changed. Using nationally defined poverty lines reflecting prevailing living standards among OECD member countries, even within the developed world, there were some 100 million people living in poverty.

The transition to advanced capitalism that has occurred in developed countries has been associated with far-reaching changes not only in the health and literacy of their populations, but also in their living costs and living standards. There is a broad distinction to be drawn between 'absolute' poverty (as a condition in which people cannot achieve physical subsistence) and 'relative' poverty (as a condition in which they cannot cope or take part in the society in which they live). Recalling the discussion in chapter 2 above, our basic human needs may be absolute, but what is required to satisfy those needs is relative to the society in which we find ourselves. To live with dignity and to have any sort of control over one's life in an advanced industrial society means having rather more than would be enough barely to feed oneself. It is unlikely (but not impossible) for people in developed countries to starve, but, according to an official EU measure that counts the number of people living in households with less than a set proportion of average income, 22 per cent of the UK population were poor at the turn of the millennium (EC 2001). 'Want' has not been defeated, but without the income that is obtained through the social security system, this figure would be very much higher.

Returning to the global stage, the United Nations' Millennium Development Goals include the targets set out in box 4.2.

Once again, these targets may be regarded as modest or ambitious depending on one's perspective. What Social Policy is concerned with, however, is the mechanisms by which poverty can be contained, whether in the developed or the developing world. While there is at least some measure of consensus in favour of health and education provision, mechanisms for income maintenance provision are contested. Of the three kinds of established welfare regime that we discussed in chapter 3, each prioritizes a different principle when it comes to social security. Liberal regimes favour selective or means-tested safety nets. Conservative regimes

Box 4.2 Millennium Development Goals and targets relating to income maintenance and employment

Goal: Eradicate extreme poverty and hunger

Targets: 'Halve, between 1990 and 2015, the proportion of people whose income is less than $1 a day.'

'Halve, between 1990 and 2015, the proportion of people who suffer from hunger.'

Source: www.un.org/millenniumgoals and see UNDP 2003.

favour social insurance or contribution-based benefits and pensions. Social Democratic regimes favour universal provision. All developed countries, in practice, combine these three principles to produce their own unique system of social security. Despite this, as we have also seen, what the 'Washington Consensus' seeks to impose on the developing world are selective 'safety nets', rather than social insurance or universal forms of provision.

Meanwhile, in the developed countries popular opinion on such matters remains ambivalent. In countries with long experience of means-tested safety nets, they can be deeply unpopular. This is because they remain associated with the stigmatizing effects of the Poor Law (see chapter 2 above). And yet the distinctions once made under the Poor Law between the deserving and the undeserving poor continue to hold sway over social attitudes. People are more supportive of public spending on pensions for old people and allowances for children than on benefits for unemployed people or lone parents (e.g. Lipsey 1994). Just as everyone accepts that they will need health and education provision at some stage in their life, so everyone hopes to grow old. And they expect that they will, by then, deserve a pension. On the other hand, people hope that in the course of their lives they will never encounter 'Idleness'. They hope never to become unemployed or to be involuntarily excluded by their personal circumstances from the labour market. And some may feel that those who fail to avoid such hazards are somehow less deserving of support. Despite this, and largely because of their dislike for means-tested social assistance, people in developed countries seem to maintain a commitment to forms of income maintenance based on social insurance. They do so it would seem reluctantly, and in opposition to their political leaders (Dean 2004a). People want some basic guarantees from the state, but they would prefer – if they should need it – to be unequivocally entitled to such support on the basis of the past contributions that they or members of their family have made.

Would it be possible to avoid poverty without publicly funded social security? In theory, it might be. There have been attempts – in Latin America, for example (see Barrientos 2004) – to construct pension systems based entirely on compulsory contributions to private pension providers. Equally, it is possible to secure private, as opposed to social, insurance arrangements against sickness at work and even unemployment. I shall discuss some of the pros and cons of such arrangements in chapter 5. In many developed countries, however – particularly when it comes to provision for old age or retirement pensions – people rely on a mixture of state and private provision. Clearly, there are people who need never rely on the state for income maintenance. The important point, however, is that the state plays a critical role in ensuring that the poor as well as the rich, unskilled workers as well as skilled workers, disabled people as well as able-bodied people are able, one way or another, to maintain their incomes if they should be unable to earn for themselves.

This brings me to the question of who benefits from income maintenance and employment policies. Do they function in the interests of the national economy or in the interests of the individual citizen? Social security provision enables people, up to a point, to withdraw from the labour market when they are too sick, too old or if they are disabled or have responsibility for caring for children or disabled relatives. Employment policies may provide social protection through minimum wage levels and maximum working hours; the regulation of health and safety at work; protection against arbitrary dismissal; the right to holidays and family-friendly working arrangements. All this clearly benefits the individual.

However, social security provision has always been mindful of the need to promote labour market incentives through the conditions that attach to the receipt of benefits (Dean 2002). Benefit for people who are unemployed may be withheld if they are voluntarily unemployed or if they have lost a job through misconduct; it may be withdrawn if claimants fail to demonstrate that they are actively seeking employment, or if they refuse the offer of a job. Benefits for people who are sick or disabled will be subject to medical conditions and may be withheld or withdrawn if it should appear that the claimant is capable of employment. Contributory retirement pensions are, in any event, dependent upon the claimant's lifetime employment record. Recent innovations in several developed countries go further (e.g. Millar 2003). These have entailed, on the one hand, a move towards the use of in-work benefits or tax-credits, which provide means-tested supplements to encourage people to take up low-wage employment; on the other, a move towards what has been characterized as 'workfare'. The term 'workfare' has been used to describe schemes in which claimants of working age are required as a condition of receiving benefits to undertake various forms of work experience or training, or to attend compulsory interviews at which their readiness to work is investigated. These developments have followed a shift, particularly in liberal welfare regimes, away from the kind of macro-economic management that created jobs in favour of policies that would make their countries' labour markets more competitive.

In this context Social Policy is concerned not only with the extent and sustainability of income maintenance and employment policy, but with the implications such policies may have in shaping everyday lives; in enabling people on the one hand, but in controlling them on the other.

Housing and the Environment

Housing and environmental policies provide the means to defeat Beveridge's other great giant, 'Squalor'. Squalor has become virtually synonymous with urbanization. I outlined in chapter 2 how the transition from feudalism to industrial capitalism was associated with population displacement and urbanization. Whereas barely 2 per cent of the world's population was urbanized in 1800, by 2000 around three quarters of the population in developed countries and nearly one half of the population of the world as a whole were urban dwellers (UN-HABITAT 2003). Rapid and uncontrolled urbanization creates 'slums', 'shanty towns' or *favelas*. While social policies have done much to alleviate slum conditions in developed countries, there remain neighbourhoods within and around many of the world's greatest cities that are characterized by deprivation and poor living conditions. It is estimated that globally there are around one billion slum dwellers and that this number could double by 2030. In the developing countries over 40 per cent of the urban population live in what are officially classified as slums and this is one of the key targets addressed by the United Nations Millennium Development Goals (see box 4.3).

It is important, of course, to remember that squalor, even if it is less visible, can and does exist in rural as well as urban contexts. 'Squalor' is an emotive, but imprecise, term. If we are to address the issue in terms of basic human needs, then there are two elements to be addressed. First, human beings need shelter. Second, they need a habitable local environment.

Adequate shelter, or housing, is clearly a requirement for good health, but housing provision poses a different set of issues to healthcare provision. What counts as adequate housing is dependent on cultural norms, and also on climatic conditions. More fundamentally, however, housing

Box 4.3 Millennium Development Goals and targets relating to housing and the environment

Goal 7: Ensure environmental sustainability

Targets: 'Have achieved by 2020 a significant improvement in the lives of at least 100 million slum dwellers.'

'Integrate the principles of sustainable development into country policies and programmes and reverse the loss of environmental resources.'

Source: www.un.org/millenniumgoals and see UNDP 2003.

requires land. Land has always been associated with power and in capitalist societies it has become a valuable, and therefore expensive, commodity. In order to ensure the provision of adequate housing, policy makers can use a range of options or levers. They can:

- Use income maintenance policies, such as those we have just discussed, in order to ensure that people can afford to rent or buy their homes.
- Use legislative powers and/or subsidies to regulate and/or support landowners to ensure that they provide an adequate supply of affordable housing.
- Retain or acquire land in order directly to provide a subsidized or relatively low-cost supply of public rented housing.

Different developed countries favour different approaches, depending on specific circumstances and priorities. The case of the UK is not necessarily typical, but it illustrates the important role that social policies can play in shaping housing arrangements (Murie 2003; Lund 1996). At the start of the twentieth century in the UK, a mere 10 per cent of the population owned their own homes. By the end of the century almost 70 per cent did so. This dramatic statistic masks a quite bizarre story, involving the use of all three of the above levers. Public housing provision was expanded, but then extensively privatized. Private landlords were regulated and then deregulated. Substantial subsidies were given, first through mortgage interest tax relief to home ownership and latterly through means-tested housing benefits for the generally impoverished minority that now remains in private or public rented accommodation. Additionally, the protection that these levers afford will not necessarily be sufficient to ensure that some vulnerable social groups are not excluded from housing provision. This may necessitate additional policies specifically addressed to combating homelessness (e.g. Daly 1996). Such policies may focus on prioritizing access to public housing for certain social groups (particularly homeless families with children), or it may focus on remedial forms of support for people living on the street.

Given the nature of land as a commodity, the policy mechanisms that determine access to housing can be especially controversial. Some see shelter, in the same way as necessities such as food and clothing, as something that in normal circumstances people should be able to secure and pay for themselves. Others see it as a uniquely important requirement from which private financiers and construction companies ought not unfairly to profit at the expense of the needy, and which ought, therefore, to be collectively guaranteed.

However, shelter alone is not enough. Human wellbeing also requires a secure and habitable environment. There are two aspects to this. The first relates to what might be termed 'social ecology'; the other to the quality of the built environment.

By social ecology I am referring to the social sustainability of a spatially defined community or neighbourhood (Wilson 1987; Lupton and Power 2002). For example, economic change may deprive a particular neighbourhood of employment opportunities. As a consequence, better-qualified middle-class residents may flee to other centres of employment. In doing so, they take with them their economic wealth and they leave behind poorer and more vulnerable residents. They deprive the community of leadership and they disrupt the social structures that had enabled the neighbourhood to cohere. The neighbourhood suffers not only high unemployment and increased poverty but also deteriorating community stability, rising crime levels and a self-reinforcing cycle of social exclusion as it acquires an unfavourable reputation in the eyes of the outside world.

If public housing is spatially concentrated this can sometimes lead to similarly adverse neighbourhood effects. This is likely to occur when public housing is reserved only for the poorest members of society and if – as has occurred both in the UK and the USA – it is allowed to become a stigmatized form of housing tenure. Such a phenomenon is by no means confined to inner urban neighbourhoods, or even to developed countries. When inner urban slum clearance programmes replace poor quality private housing with badly serviced public housing schemes in peripheral out-of-town locations, these neighbourhoods too can develop problems (Power 1999). Economic pressures, ill-advised housing policies or a combination of such factors can create social environments that are not sustainable. In some circumstances it can lead to situations, as in the north of England, where tracts of urban housing are virtually abandoned at a time of housing shortages in the south. This is the point at which new kinds of urban regeneration policy may be brought into play; policies that seek to promote community participation as well as attracting various forms of economic investment to a troubled or abandoned neighbourhood (e.g. Atkinson 2003).

Often alongside urban regeneration initiatives, Local Agenda 21 projects may also play a role in seeking to ensure the environmental sustainability of local planning and development. Local Agenda 21 was the creation of the UN environmental summit in Rio in 1992 and has become the vehicle by which the second of the Millennium Development Goal targets in box 4.3 can be addressed at local level (Cahill 2002).

Stepping back in time for a moment, urban planning policy has long sought to address issues to do with the built environment: with physical infrastructure on the one hand and with the design and quality of housing on the other. What had been regarded as public health concerns can now be seen to intersect with environmental concerns. We saw in chapter 2 that public health policies first emerged in the industrialized world during the nineteenth century, when the primary concern was sanitation. In later years, however, and particularly since the Second World War, urban planning has been concerned with the regulation of the built environment with regard to its aesthetic appearance, but also with regard to matters of population density and the separation of residential and industrial land use. In the past such regulation has failed to prevent – or, in parts of the world, has even encouraged – such innovations as high-rise residential housing schemes that have proved deeply unpopular with residents and have helped to create some of the unsustainable social environments referred to above. However, building control and environmental health legislation can and (in the UK certainly) has been used to raise the standards of construction, maintenance and management of both private and public sector housing (e.g. Dean 2002: ch. 7).

Nevertheless, the challenge for Social Policy is not only about 'bricks and mortar' (to use a distinctively English colloquialism). It is important that the quantity and quality of the housing that is available to meet human needs should be sufficient. But it is also important that people should be able to afford access to housing, that it should be in the right place and that it should provide a suitable and sustainable social environment.

The 'Personal' Social Services

In the UK the personal social services are sometimes described as the 'fifth' social service (after health, education, social security and housing) and often as the Cinderella services. Beveridge did not identify a giant to be slain by these services, because they are concerned not with the needs that everybody inevitably has, but with the special needs of vulnerable people. They are the kind of services that are delivered or managed by professional social workers. Describing the personal social services in this way invites two kinds of misunderstanding.

The first is primarily terminological. In many countries trained social workers are responsible for administering social assistance benefits. For the purposes of this chapter, however, I have treated social assistance as a component of income maintenance. It needs to be recognized that professional 'personal' support for highly needy social groups is sometimes linked to social assistance administration, especially where there is a discretionary human service element to social assistance (e.g. Hall and Midgley 2004: ch. 7). Similarly, social workers in all parts of the world may have a key role in providing support for homeless people, or, for example, in facilitating community involvement in urban regeneration initiatives, activities that I have addressed separately. The second potential misunderstanding is that personal social services are merely residual; that they are a miscellany of relatively marginal 'social welfare' services; or that they are leftovers from the Poor Law era. This misses the point. All human beings are vulnerable. During childhood they are vulnerable to abuse. In the course of, or throughout, their lives they may experience disability, mental health problems or learning difficulties. As they grow old, they may become frail and disabled. In such circumstances, it is the function of the personal social services to ensure protection and care. If there is nobody there to protect or to care for them, then anybody might at some point need personal social services.

Precisely because they are 'personal', the personal social services bear upon how people manage their lives. This raises a host of issues upon which I can only touch (but for illustrative materials see Baldock 2003; Denney 1996). Let me first take services for children and young people. The primary objective of services is to protect children and young people from physical, mental or sexual exploitation or abuse; to ensure they are able properly to develop; to help control those who may be 'delinquent' or have behavioural problems. To this end social workers may be involved in:

- supporting or counselling families with children, including and particularly where children are identified as being in need, or at risk;
- overseeing all forms of non-family-based childcare provision;
- removing children from families or situations in which they are at risk;

- organizing or providing alternative foster or residential care for children;
- supervising children who have been engaged in illegal or dangerous activities.

Any kind of intervention in respect of the care and control of children or young people entails judgements about the best interests of the child. Such judgements are always difficult and often sensitive. They must, to an extent, be informed by specific norms or assumptions about what is acceptable. Adults may, for example, believe that their treatment of children in their care is sanctioned by their particular class, cultural or religious background. Who is to say that a professional social worker's conception of what constitutes good parenting or childcare practice has universal validity? But, on the other hand, the obligation imposed on the personal social services is to protect children or young people from treatment or from situations that are manifestly harmful.

Turning for a moment to services for adults, the personal social services are concerned with the provision of 'social care'. Social care may entail the provision of residential homes or day centres for people who cannot adequately care for themselves, or it may entail provision that facilitates what is fashionably termed 'care in the community'. Care in the community is a protean term that may on the one hand refer to small group homes in which younger disabled people or people with learning difficulties look after themselves with some element of supervision. On the other hand, it may refer to domiciliary care services provided to a frail elderly person living in her or his own home. There are at least three issues that Social Policy has to address:

The limits of care in the community. The call for care in the community may be construed as a call to limit policy intervention in social care. I shall return to this issue in chapter 9. For now, the point to be made is that everywhere in the world most social care actually takes place in the community; or, more specifically, it is performed by the community. It is undertaken at home by family members. Depending on the circumstances, this can represent the very best or the very worst form of care (see Qureshi and Walker 1989). It is important to recognize that there are difficult situations in which it is fairer and safer for care to be provided by professional carers, rather than by family members.

The health/social care boundary. An enduring issue, particularly in the English context, is that the provision of healthcare and social care tend to be organized by separate institutions. People who are chronically frail or disabled may require intensive care (including assistance with feeding and bathing, for example), although this may entail no specialized medical treatment. The implication is that it can be absurdly difficult to determine how their care should be organized and paid for. More fundamentally, it presents an ethical problem since there is a risk that certain forms of long-term palliative care – because the skills they require tend to be undervalued – can become marginalized or neglected.

Social care vs. independent living. In recent years the independent living movement has mounted a global campaign to ensure that disabled people should be enabled, so far as possible, to live independent lives. This presents a challenge to conventional notions of social care (e.g. Morris 2003). The argument is that personal social services should be less concerned with the direct provision of care and more concerned with the provision of resources for disabled people to control by themselves.

The personal social services have to address issues of human wellbeing in some of the most extreme or highly particular circumstances. It is for that reason that they provide what is in some ways one of the most interesting areas of study within Social Policy.

Summary

This chapter has considered what human wellbeing entails by outlining the main areas of social policy or human service provision with which Social Policy, as an academic subject, is concerned:

- First, it has discussed health and education provision. These services are often regarded as the bedrock of the welfare states of the developed world and as the priority for social development in the developing world. Health and education are essential components of our basic human needs. However, there is a variety of ways in which such provision can be financed and organized. Additionally, public provision to meet such needs may be fashioned to benefit national and economic as well as individual interests. The chapter has considered some of the changing and competing priorities that such services must encompass and how health and education provision may not be of equal benefit to all social groups.
- Second, it has discussed income maintenance and employment. Under capitalism most people – whether as wage earners or as dependent family members – must directly or indirectly depend on employment.

Failing that, they must depend on income maintenance systems for the basic means of subsistence. Governments may seek to sustain the level of employment in the national economy but can also use tax and social security systems in order to prevent or relieve the poverty of those not in employment. Once again, there is a variety of ways in which such provision can be financed and organized. And once again provision to meet such needs may be fashioned to benefit national and economic as well as individual interests. The chapter has considered some of the different principles that may be used to inform social security provision and ways in which the conditions attaching to such provision may assist the functioning of labour markets.

- Third, it has discussed housing and the environment. The world is becoming increasingly urban and the uncontrolled growth of cities can bring housing and environmental problems. Human beings need shelter, but they also need a sustainably habitable environment. The chapter has considered the ways in which governments can try and ensure that people have access to suitable and affordable housing, the ways in which adverse housing environments can be created and the ways in which the quality of housing and the built environment can be improved.
- Finally, it has discussed the personal social services. These are services provided to especially vulnerable people. They include provision for the protection of children from abuse and social care services for disabled and frail elderly people. The chapter has considered just some of the sensitive issues associated with the kinds of intervention that such services make in people's lives.

5

Who Gets What?

In this chapter we shall have the first of several encounters with one of the key concepts for Social Policy, namely social justice. Social justice is concerned with who gets what in society, and whether it is 'right' or 'fair'. For the moment, I shall be leaving to one side the moral and ethical dimensions of the question and shall approach it instead primarily from an economic viewpoint. Social Policy as a subject is not driven by economics, but economics can be important. I want, first of all, to consider the concept of 'public goods' and the different ways in which they can be shared. Second, I shall discuss where the money may come from to pay for social policy provision. Third, I shall be examining the various underlying principles that may inform the distribution of social resources. And finally, I shall outline the different ways in which welfare states may achieve social redistribution in practice.

The focus of the chapter will be mainly on how welfare states have functioned in developed countries, but the principles involved have a wide and generic application.

Sharing Public Goods

If Social Policy is concerned with provision for human need, economics is concerned with the allocation of scarce resources (Gough 2003; Le Grand et al. 1992). Before the emergence of economics as a branch of the social sciences, philosophers had studied what was called 'political economy'. In some ways, political economy provided a more holistic perspective than modern economics, since it sought to address the political dynamics of economic processes. It addressed the problem of how to produce and supply the goods and services on which human wellbeing depends, in the right quantities and at the right time. How do we balance production with consumption; supply with demand; effort with gain; costs with benefits? And how can this be achieved at a collective or 'aggregate', not just an individual, level. When Daniel Defoe's fictional character, Robinson Crusoe, lived all alone on his desert island, these balancing acts were relatively straightforward. But the appearance of Man Friday introduced a whole new dynamic; the dynamic that results as soon as people have to co-operate or compete with one another. It is that dynamic in which we are interested.

Political economy has been dominated by two competing traditions: the classical and the critical. The classical tradition, associated with Adam Smith (1776) and David Ricardo (1817), is preoccupied with the way that market forces operate. It assumes that the *value* of the goods that human beings require reflects the amount of labour that goes into producing them, but that their *price* will be determined by the market. If the market is left to its own devices the price mechanism, like an 'invisible hand', will ensure that equilibrium is achieved: everybody will be able to buy the things they need at or about a price that reflects what they are worth. The balancing act is performed by the market. The implication, however, is that things will go wrong if we interfere with the market; and, in particular, if we involve the state in the provision of goods that are marketable (Bacon and Eltis 1976). Classical political economy recognizes that there are such things as 'public goods' – goods such as public health and policing that benefit not just individuals but society as a whole – but it insists that these should be provided by the state only if they are not by their nature marketable. In providing public goods, the primary role of the state should in effect be the prevention or control of what might be termed 'public bads'; that is external effects, such as pollution, that might be caused by private producers; or problems such as epidemics, social disorder and crime. When public service provision steps outside these bounds, it becomes excessive; it crowds out the private production of goods and threatens the economic equilibrium upon which human wellbeing depends.

The critical tradition, associated with Karl Marx (1887), is premised on a critique of capitalism. It argues that the labour that goes into producing goods for human consumption produces *surplus* value, unrelated to the usefulness of the goods, and this drives a remorseless process of capital accumulation. The system is based on social exploitation and, far from securing a natural equilibrium, has an inherent tendency to crisis. It is because of this tendency that capitalism depends on state intervention (e.g. Gough 1979). State investment in health and education increases the productivity of labour. State provision of benefits and services reduces the living costs of workers and the wages that employers must pay. The beneficial effects of state intervention help to legitimize capitalism, to conceal its exploitative nature, and so maintain social order.

Each tradition, taken to its extreme, is reflected in a different political ideology. The classical tradition is reflected in the kind of economic liberalism or neo-liberalism that favours completely unfettered markets. The critical tradition was reflected in Soviet-style state socialism, which sought to replace capitalism with a centrally planned economy, in which all goods were produced and distributed as if they were public goods. The evidence, however, suggests that neither unfettered markets nor state planning can be relied upon. Without state intervention, markets fail to meet everybody's needs, and this leads to unsustainable social inequalities. In the absence of market forces, on the other hand, state planning tends to break down under the volume of information that is necessary to ensure that everybody's needs are met. The creation of the capitalist welfare state was based on a compromise; the combination of a 'managed' market with a 'mixed' economy (that includes both private and public elements). The compromise was informed by the thinking of the economist, John Maynard Keynes (1936). The new orthodoxy – that came to be known as Keynesianism – endorsed the principles of economic regulation and a protectionist welfare state; it aimed for full employment and was tolerant of inflation; it favoured maintained public spending and 'demand-side management' (the manipulation of public spending to stimulate or restrain consumption). Keynesianism was a central tenet of the social liberalism that informed the welfare state as it had been originally envisaged by Beveridge (see chapter 2 above).

Associated, however, with the process of economic globalization (that we discussed in chapter 3) was an alternative economic orthodoxy, called monetarism. Monetarism repudiated the Keynesian compromise in favour of a revamped version of classical political economy. This is an orthodoxy that endorses the principles of economic deregulation and emphasizes national competitiveness, rather than social protectionism; it is tolerant of unemployment, but aims to control inflation by restricting the money supply (through the control of interest rates); it favours restricted public spending and 'supply-side management' (policies that stimulate productivity, not consumption). Monetarist economic theory was forced onto the political agenda in the 1980s by leaders such as Ronald Reagan and Margaret Thatcher. In fact, monetarism has never been that rigorously practised by the rich nations, especially in the USA, which continues to run substantial budget deficits. But the tenets of monetarism continue to be called in aid of demands to limit social spending. Elements of monetarism have remained as part of the new 'Third Way' compromises forged in the 1990s by political leaders such as Bill Clinton, Tony Blair and Gerhard Schroeder (Lewis and Surender 2004). It represents one of the key elements of the so-called 'Washington Consensus' that we discussed in chapter 3, which informs the basis of the conditions upon which the world's international financial institutions offer assistance to developing countries.

This (partial) return to the principles of classical political economy is of particular significance to Social Policy. On a strict monetarist interpretation, the state should be allowed to provide only the kinds of goods or amenities that nobody can be excluded from using, and which could never under normal circumstances be produced privately for sale. So, for example, the state might be permitted to provide public sewage systems (or, at least, to commission them under public/private partnership arrangements) so as to *prevent* disease, but the market should be the preferred method for providing individual healthcare services in order to *treat* disease. In practice, all sorts of compromises may be struck in terms of the balance between state and market provision of public goods, and I shall discuss this further in chapter 9. The point for now, however, is that Social Policy is concerned with the basis on which public goods can be shared. We saw in chapter 4 how the main services that welfare states organize tend, in whole or in part, to be public goods. They usually serve to benefit society as a whole, at the same time as benefiting the individual. They are services upon which – with or without state involvement – human wellbeing will depend, at both an individual and a collective level. Where we share collectively in the benefits of a public good, how – as individuals – should we contribute to the production of that good?

Where's the Money?

This brings us to the question of how the kinds of human services that are discussed in chapter 4 can, in fact, be paid for. If, once again, we take the UK as an example, it has been calculated that, in one way or another, roughly half the nation's annual income (or Gross Domestic Product) is spent on human services (Burchardt et al. 1999). A great deal of this is paid for privately, but we have already seen in chapter 1 that, in 2004–5, around £320 billion – just over a quarter of the UK's Gross Domestic Product or GDP – was to be met out of public spending (see table 1.1). In other words, in the UK around a half of the human services we require are paid for collectively through social spending. In this respect, the UK – like all developed countries – still has a mixed economy.

In other countries, public finance accounts for a greater share and, in other countries, a lesser share.

Our concern for now, however, is with how public finances function. Sticking with the UK as our example, it may be seen from table 5.1 where most of the money for the planned expenditure outlined in table 1.1 was to come from. The shortfall would be met, if needs be, from government borrowing. As ever, the UK is not necessarily typical, but table 5.1 helps to illustrate the different ways in which taxes can be raised. Benjamin Franklin, the eighteenth-century American statesman, once wrote that 'in this world nothing can be said to be certain, except death and taxes' (1789). Broadly speaking, taxes can be raised in three ways: from individuals, from consumption, or from enterprises (Glennerster 2003a; 2003b).

There are two principal ways in which individual incomes may be taxed: by income tax, or by way of national insurance contributions (sometimes called social security contributions) that are compulsorily

Table 5.1 UK government revenues 2004–5 (projected)

	£ billion	% total revenue	% GDP
Individual taxes			
Income tax	128	28	11
National Insurance Contributions[a]	78	17	7
Local council tax	20	4	2
Consumption taxes			
Value Added Tax (VAT)	73	16	6
Excise duties	40	9	3
Enterprise taxes[a]			
Corporation tax	35	8	3
Business rates	19	4	2
Other income (inc. capital taxes, charges, proceeds from asset sales, etc.)	62	14	5
Total revenue	455	100	39

[a] National Insurance Contributions (sometimes called Social Security Contributions or SSCs) are paid both by employees and employers. Arguably, the employers' element might be included as a business and not a personal tax. Whether the cost of employer SSCs are met by employers or whether, as an element of their wage costs, they are borne in effect by employees is something of a moot point.

Source: http://budget2004.treasury.gov.uk/page_09.html (Crown Copyright) and see HM Treasury 2004a.

deducted from people's wages. I shall shortly return to discuss the different principles that inform each kind of arrangement, but for now we may regard things like national insurance or social security contributions as an example of what is sometimes called a hypothecated tax: a tax that is levied for a specific rather than a general purpose. Based on recent OECD data (OECD 2003), people on an average wage in the UK would expect in total to pay 33 per cent of their earnings in taxes, whereas if they were in the USA they would pay just 29 per cent, but in Germany they would have to pay 58 per cent. Additionally, in the UK, people must currently pay a form of local taxation – the council tax – based on the value of the property they occupy, although the overall contribution that this makes to the public finances is relatively small. There are many different forms of local tax. During the 1980s in the UK there was a short-lived and deeply unpopular attempt to reintroduce a form of poll tax: a fixed tax payable by every resident. In some countries, local services are financed by levying a local income tax, rather than a property or residency tax. Overall, however, it may be seen that in the UK getting on for a half of all public finances are raised though taxes on individuals.

An alternative way of raising public revenues is by taxing not what people earn, but what they consume. The advantage of this is that it leaves people freer to spend their money as they choose. The disadvantage is that people who have little money and little choice may end up paying out a disproportionate amount in taxes. In practice, all developed countries use a mixture of individual and consumption taxes. Consumption taxes can be levied directly on consumer spending through purchase or value added taxes, or indirectly through excise duties or tariffs that are charged to the producers or importers of goods. The disadvantages of consumption taxes can be mitigated by charging lower levels of tax on essential produce, and higher levels on luxury goods (or, for example, on harmful products, such as tobacco). Historically, some countries, such as the USA, have in the past relied very heavily on public revenues from charges on imported goods, a practice that has often had a significant impact on world trading patterns. In the case of the UK, something less than a quarter of government revenue is obtained through consumption taxes.

Taxes on corporate enterprises or businesses can be levied against their profits and additionally by way of charges for local infrastructural services (which, in the UK, is currently achieved by a business rate charged on the value of the premises occupied by an enterprise). The level of taxes on enterprises in the UK is currently relatively low, contributing little more than one tenth of the overall cost of public services. The basic corporate tax rate is just 30 per cent, compared with 39 per cent in the

USA and 40 per cent in Germany (OECD 2003). It is by having low corporate tax rates that countries hope to attract inward investment. In general, the proportion of taxes that developed countries seek to levy from corporate enterprise has, since the 1970s, been declining (see Gough 2000).

The greater part of the cost of collectively provided human services is met from taxes on what people earn and spend. However, insofar as individuals may get back more or less from the welfare state than they contribute, the key issue from a Social Policy perspective is the distributive or redistributive effects of the process.

Principles of Distribution

When a substantial part of the resources that are required to meet human needs is collectively administered, how should those resources be allocated? In chapter 2 we explored some of the ideological influences that have inevitably been brought to bear in considering such a question, and in chapter 3 we considered the various ways in which different countries have addressed the question in practice. But here, from a strictly logical perspective, I intend to address three fundamental, but interrelated, questions of principle. Should publicly administered resources be distributed:

Universally or selectively? If a welfare state is acting on behalf of the community at large, it can distribute resources on the same basis to every member of that community, or it may operate selectively, providing resources only to those who need or deserve help. A case can be made on efficiency grounds for either approach. If benefits and services are available on the same basis to everybody, this ensures that everybody is guaranteed the necessary minimum level of help to secure their wellbeing; because everybody gets the same, no stigma can attach to receiving that help and nobody need be deterred from seeking help; and those people who do not need the help they receive will, if the system is funded by progressive taxation, be able to pay back what they have received, as well as contributing to the help received by other members of the community. If, on the other hand, benefits and services are made available only to those who need or deserve them, this will ensure that such resources as are available will be put to the most effective use; optimum rather than minimum levels of help may be afforded to those in the greatest need; those people who do not require help will neither be deterred from helping themselves, nor made resentful by unnecessarily high levels of taxation.

On the basis of entitlement or discretion? Resources may be allocated in accordance with a system of rules or a legal framework on the one hand, or at the discretion of expert administrators or professionals on the other. Once again, a reasoned case can be made for either approach. If access to public resources is governed on the basis of entitlement, this makes the allocation process calculable and predictable; it ensures that help cannot be withheld corruptly or on the basis of subjective prejudices; it means that social provision becomes – as discussed in chapter 2 above – a component of our citizenship. If, on the other hand, access to public resources is governed by discretion, it makes the allocation process more accurate and effective; it means that the complex and specific needs of individuals can be met; it ensures that social provision does not become embroiled in unnecessary legal technicality and conflict.

On a demand-led or a rationed basis? Resources may be allocated in response to the level of demand for human services, or – where resources are limited – access will have to be rationed. This dichotomy overlaps with the two I have just mentioned. An expansive welfare state might elect for universal and/or entitlement-based forms of resource allocation and a large social policy budget. A more restrictive welfare state might elect for selective and/or discretionary forms of resource allocation and a smaller social policy budget. In practice, of course, even the most generous welfare states are subject to budget limits and even the most parsimonious may have to respond to unforeseen levels of need. For example, in countries where public healthcare provision is free at the point of use, it may be necessary to restrict access to new and expensive forms of medical treatment. And in countries where benefits for unemployed people are made rigorously selective, it may still be difficult to contain the costs of provision when unemployment rises during a recession. The equation is complicated, however. On the one hand, universal provision may have to be set at an inadequate level in order to limit the cost, while rules intended to guarantee entitlement to resources may be framed or interpreted in restrictive ways. On the other hand, selective benefits if they are set at an adequate level and meet the needs of significant numbers of people can become expensive, while beneficent administrators and autonomous professionals may exercise discretion with excessive generosity.

These basic questions, and their potentially complex answers, each deserve an introductory chapter of their own. For now, however, I shall conclude by illustrating how principles of distribution apply in the real world of policy making and social provision.

How does it All Pan Out?

Every welfare regime has its own story to tell when it comes to how effective it is in distributing resources to meet human need. However, whatever the ostensible aims of policy makers, the job of Social Policy as an academic subject is to understand how distributive processes actually work.

Distributive effects can be either 'vertical' or 'horizontal'. They may serve to redistribute from people at the top of the wealth and income distribution to those at the bottom. Alternatively, they may serve to redistribute resources across the community as a whole. Vertical redistribution has an equalizing effect: like Robin Hood, it robs the rich to pay the poor. Horizontal redistribution has a smoothing effect: like a savings bank, it doesn't necessarily transfer resources from one group of people to another, but allows people over the course of their lives to pay in when they have money, and to draw out when they don't (e.g. Hills 2003).

To illustrate this, let us revisit the ways in which different social security systems work (see chapter 4). A selective or means-tested benefits system that only pays benefits to the poor is ostensibly more likely to achieve vertical redistribution than a social insurance or contributory benefits system. However, unless the benefits that are paid are reasonably generous and the taxes that pay for them are collected primarily from the rich, the redistributive effect may be quite small, and the impact on the degree of inequality in society might be quite limited. A social insurance or contributory benefits system that pays benefits to anybody who has made the necessary contributions is ostensibly more likely to achieve horizontal distribution than a selective or means-tested benefits system. However, depending on the rules of the scheme, low-income earners in times of need may benefit substantially from funds contributed primarily by high-income earners. We cannot make assumptions about how things will pan out in practice.

The distributive effects of tax and social security are more obvious than those of other human services. None the less, what has been called the 'social wage' (see Land 1992) encompasses the overall value of all publicly provided services, including, for example, public healthcare and state education. When people receive health and education services in kind, the value of those services can be imputed in terms of what they would otherwise have had to pay for those services. The UK's Office for National Statistics undertakes an annual study to determine the effects of taxes and benefits on household income and this demonstrates that in the UK poorer households benefit more from state intervention than richer households. According to the latest figures available at the time of writing, in 2002–3 the combined effect of taxes and welfare benefits (including the imputed value of health and education provision) was almost a fourfold reduction of the gap between the richest fifth of the population and the poorest fifth (Lakin 2004). But if we remember that people on higher incomes in effect pay back some or all of the value of the benefits and services they receive, the important thing to understand is what the overall effect of government intervention is over a person's lifetime. Using a computer simulation model, Jane Falkingham and John Hills (1995) have estimated that in the UK roughly a quarter of the redistribution resulting from government intervention is 'Robin Hood' redistribution and three quarters is 'savings-bank' redistribution.

We must be careful when interpreting these kinds of data, which necessarily rely on all sorts of assumptions about household needs and about how different social groups might access public services. Although aspects of his research have since been called into question, Julian Le Grand (1982) made an important contribution to debate when he argued that in the UK it was the middle classes in society, and not the poor, who were reaping the greatest benefits from services such as healthcare, education, housing and transport. It can be better-off people who get the best deal from the welfare state if, compared to poorer people, they make more effective use of health services; if their children remain for longer within the education system; if they receive substantial tax concessions that reduce the costs of their housing; if, as private motorists, they do not have to meet the full costs of building and maintaining the roads. Le Grand suggested that the welfare state had been failing to deliver a 'strategy of equality'. But this begs the question – was there ever a strategy of equality in the first place? Can we assume that welfare states achieve equitable outcomes? Le Grand alerts us to a present danger that some forms of social policy provision may fuel, not abate, certain kinds of inequality. However, most welfare states – including, as we have seen, the UK – do succeed in at least limiting the extent of social inequality in their societies. At the same time, an important feature of most welfare states is that at least some of the resources they dispense on society's behalf are not intended, in Alan Deacon and Jonathan Bradshaw's words, to be 'reserved for the poor' (1983) but to enhance everybody's wellbeing.

Summary

This chapter has explored some of the economic dimensions of Social Policy. It has outlined four main concerns:

- Every society has to produce the goods that are necessary for human wellbeing and distribute them among its members. In complex societies this can be left to the self-regulating mechanisms of a free market economy, or it can be entrusted to state control. The chapter has discussed how different compromises between these approaches have evolved and how, in particular, the production of 'public goods' may be affected.
- Insofar as it is necessary or desirable for some of the goods essential for human wellbeing to be collectively produced, there have to be ways of collectively paying for them. The chapter has illustrated how taxes to fund human services may be levied upon individuals, upon consumption and upon enterprises.
- When resources are collectively administered, principles are required to govern the distribution of those resources. The chapter has outlined some of the key questions of principle that have to be considered. Should resources be shared universally, or distributed selectively to those who need them? Should their distribution be governed by rules of entitlement or by properly exercised discretion? Should they be distributed in accordance with prevailing levels of demand, or should they be rationed up to a fixed level?
- Whatever principles are applied, the distributive effects can be complex and subtle. The chapter has investigated the difference between vertical and horizontal distributional outcomes; it has illustrated the ways in which these may be combined in practice; and it has raised questions about the extent and nature of the equity that may be achieved as a consequence.

6

Who's in Control?

The last chapter was about money. I was explaining how Social Policy draws on elements of economics in order to understand who gets what in society. This chapter is about power. I shall be explaining how Social Policy draws on elements of political science in order to understand who controls the policy process. It is about much more than the rituals of party politics, because power is exercised at a variety of different levels and in a variety of different ways. I shall start by outlining some theories of power and the role of the state. I shall then take a look at how power can be exercised, first, at the local level – the level at which social policies are actually implemented or delivered; second, at the national level – the level at which social policies are supposedly decided; third, at the supra-national or regional level – the level at which wider objectives may be formulated.

The Problem of Power

Power is an elusive concept. Power can be thought of as the capacity that some human beings possess to control others. It operates at every level within human society: for example, at the military level or at the macro-economic level at one extreme, all the way down to the local community level and the dynamics of interpersonal relationships at the other. Because it may be exercised by the strong over the weak, power can surely be inimical to human wellbeing. However, power is inherent to the social policy-making process.

In chapter 2 I made clear that Social Policy as a subject has emerged from the analysis of capitalist welfare states. One of the earliest explanations and defences of the democratic capitalist state was that provided by the sociologist Max Weber (1914). His argument was that effective government requires political authority. And, to have authority is to have *more* than power. If governments are to exercise authority – and, for example, to have control over the military and the police – their power must be legitimate. Weber suggested that, historically speaking, there had been various ways in which governments had obtained or retained their legitimacy. Some governments had depended on the traditional loyalties of their subjects, others on the charismatic appeal of their leaders. But the modern capitalist era was characterized by a new kind of governance founded on rationality and rational obedience to authority. The legitimacy of the state flowed from the idea that there should be some separation of powers between:

- the legislature – a democratically elected body that debates policy and makes laws;
- an executive – the government of the day and the official apparatuses that implement the laws passed by the legislature; and
- a judiciary – the judges who independently adjudicate whether laws have been correctly interpreted and applied.

This system of checks and balances ensured the rule of law. Most importantly, this system of governance ensured predictable decision making by accountable bureaucracies and made modern social policy and administration possible.

Critics of this argument have pointed out that the inherent instability of capitalist economies can threaten the legitimacy of rational democratic governance (e.g. Habermas 1976). What is more, Weber's account addresses only the most visible part of the political and decision-making process. It fails to account for the exclusion of those voices that are never heard within what C. P. Snow (1964), in the title of a famous novel, called the 'corridors of power'. Stephen Lukes (1974) has therefore outlined what he calls a three-dimensional account of political power. In addition to the overt ways in which political conflicts and policy debates may be resolved, he points first to covert conflicts and to the processes by which political agendas are set. Just as important as the decisions that are made by policy makers are the decisions they *don't* make: the issues that are never discussed, because the voices of those whom they affect are suppressed. Second, Lukes points to what he calls 'latent' conflicts and the ways in which those in power may shape social attitudes and perceptions. Some voices remain unheard not because they have been

Box 6.1 Perspectives on powerlessness

- Karl Marx (1887) argued that capitalism has the power to distort the consciousness of the working class in ways that makes it blind to its own exploitation.
- Later commentators, such as Antonio Gramsci (1971), developed the concept of 'hegemony': a term that captures the sense in which interpretations of the world that are held in common by the dominant class in society tend to eclipse the alternative interpretations of subordinate classes. Hegemony may be achieved through education, through the press and broadcasting media, and through the general moulding of popular culture.
- More recently post-structuralist theorists, such as Michel Foucault (1979), have suggested that power is 'immanent' within all human relationships and that – although they have not been politically contrived – distinctive strategies or 'technologies' of power have evolved, technologies that determine in sometimes quite subtle ways the behaviour we all regard as 'normal'.

suppressed, but because they were never raised to start with; because people unquestioningly accept the status quo. The extent to which some people remain powerless has been explained in several different ways (see box 6.1, for example) but the important issue from a Social Policy perspective is that powerlessness negates human wellbeing.

If we return to what *can* be observed within the corridors of power, we also need to address certain competing concepts of the state (Hill 2003; Bochel and Bochel 2004). The state is to be understood as more than just 'the government'; it is that whole array of institutions through which political power is exercised and through which policies are conceived and implemented. I shall focus on three main concepts:

The pluralist view. The mainstream pluralist conception looks upon the state as the embodiment of the ideals of representative liberal democracy. Free and fair elections ensure that a plurality of voices can be heard within a legislature, so power is distributed amongst the whole electorate. Additionally, the executive and the policy-making process as a whole is open to lobbying by a variety of special interest and pressure groups (ranging, in the UK for example, from the Child Poverty Action Group to the British Medical Association) that can play an important role in influencing the development of policy. However, even the most optimistic supporters of the pluralist concept have to concede that representative democracy leaves some voices unheard, while the openness of the policy process to lobbying leaves it susceptible to the influence of those best organized or with the loudest voices. There are certain neo-Marxists for whom the state represents a 'condensation' of competing class powers (Poulantzas 1980), albeit that the end result is likely to be in the interests of the capitalist system. Conversely, there are public choice theorists who fear that, under a pluralist system, competition by electoral representatives for votes has the effect of ratcheting up public spending in a way that is economically unsustainable and is therefore damaging to capitalism.

The elitist view. The elitist conception looks behind the democratic facade of the liberal state and argues that it serves the interests of a socially defined political elite. In a classic study C. Wright Mills (1956) demonstrated that the USA was effectively controlled by the members of a relatively small and tight-knit group of leading families who occupied key positions within the political, administrative, military, commercial and industrial establishments. Similarly, in the UK, there is an enduring preponderance of an independent school and Oxford or Cambridge educated elite within all these establishments. Once again proponents of the elitist concept come from different points of the ideological compass. Some Marxists complain that the state elite directly represents the interests of the capitalist class. Some Liberals complain that key state functionaries *within* the state administrative elite are effectively subverting the democratic process.

The corporatist view. This concept tends to be associated with mainland continental European traditions in which the state acts as a broker between the major power blocs within society at large. In the modern era, these are likely to be the government itself and the peak organizations of both capital (the business sector) and labour (the trade unions). Although there had been a few official tripartite bodies in the UK prior to the 1980s (such as the National Economic and Development Council), they were always relatively marginal to the political process and have since disappeared. As we saw in chapter 3, however, corporatism is an important influence in certain welfare regimes. Additionally, we shall see in chapter 9 that there is, for example, a move in the UK and elsewhere towards the delegation of certain state functions to non-elected quasi-autonomous governmental organizations (QUANGOs), often composed of business and community sector representatives as well as central and local government officials. Some commentators suggest that this represents a new form of corporatism existing alongside the ostensibly pluralist state (Cawson and Saunders 1983).

Whichever view of the state one adopts, the question for Social Policy is how far and in what ways is the state necessary for human wellbeing? From the perspective of the classical liberal economists (see chapter 5), the answer would be that the state, though necessary to the preservation of law and order and the protection of private property, should not be allowed to become an unnecessary encumbrance upon the beneficent functioning of a free market. More recent communitarian critiques (Hadley and Hatch 1981) would suggest that the *dirigiste* nature of the modern state – its inflexible and monolithic nature – is a constraint upon, not an aid to, the self-organizing and self-supporting capacity of communities within civil society. I shall return in chapter 9 to consider how the role of the state has been called into question. For now, however, I want to illustrate how the state functions in practice.

Street-level Organization and Local Governance

We tend to think of the power of the state as something that flows downwards from national institutions. However, I have deliberately chosen to start this account at the local not the national level. Social policies, by their nature, are concerned with everyday lives. They function at 'street level'. The administration of social policies may bear upon the very fabric of the environment and the homes in which we live; the care we receive within our homes or within locally based institutions; the services and benefits that are available or that may be accessed from within the community or locality where we live. The administrators and professionals who deliver public services are in direct contact with the people they serve – in a variety of local offices, centres, surgeries, hospitals and schools, and sometimes in people's own homes. In theory, at least, their roles are determined and their conduct is governed by social policies. In practice, of course, they may exercise power of their own.

Social Policy as an academic subject is interested in how the staff who deliver 'front-line' services operate and how they interpret their roles. Michael Lipsky (1980), on the basis of a study of welfare administrators in the USA, coined the term 'street-level bureaucrats'. He demonstrated that though these administrators were usually highly committed to their jobs, in order to get by on a day-to-day basis, they would often have to develop short cuts; to develop their own rules or to bend the interpretation of the rules within which they were supposed to operate. Real life does not always fit the rules handed down by policy makers. Policy implementation is in the hands of clerks, administrators, care workers, nurses, doctors, teachers, housing officers, social workers and others. The way that policies work in practice may depend as much on the ethos and understanding of such staff as it does upon the intentions of policy makers.

Additionally, the superior knowledge and specialist expertise of certain professional human service providers places them in a potentially powerful position in relation to service users, especially when service users may be vulnerable or relatively powerless. This 'normative power' (Clarke and Newman 1997: 63) is premised on the claim that the doctor or the teacher always knows best. As we shall see in chapter 9, the site of normative power may currently be shifting in some welfare regimes from welfare professionals to local managers. Nevertheless, street-level service providers – whether they are administrators, professionals or managers – continue to exercise their own kinds of power.

With this in mind, let us turn to the structures within which front-line staff may operate. It is impossible satisfactorily to summarize the vast array of constitutional and administrative arrangements to be found in different countries. In all countries there is an important distinction to be drawn between central government, on the one hand, and local or territorial government, on the other. Additionally, there is an important distinction to be drawn between government (that is the constitutional responsibility of some central or local executive body) and governance (the processes by which policy is implemented, which may entail a variety of actors). In many countries – as much in the developed as in the developing world – voluntary sector or non-governmental organizations (NGOs), as well as government, are involved at a local level in the delivery of human services. Because of the ways in which they may be funded and the co-operative links they have with government, NGOs may sometimes function as a direct extension of, rather than as a substitute or supplement for, state apparatuses (e.g. Deakin 2003).

A broad distinction can be made between the arrangements in federal as opposed to unitary states. In the USA and in Germany, for example, the individual States or *Länder* respectively enjoy a degree of autonomy from the federal or central government, and policies and practices in different parts of the country may vary. In certain areas of social policy, federal or central government may provide a framework or set a budget, but the States or Länder are free to interpret or to apply these in different ways. There are additionally other areas of policy over which the States and Länder have complete control.

The UK, by contrast, has until quite recently been a strictly unitary state, in which all policy was determined by central government. Indeed, local government can still undertake only such tasks as it is expressly empowered to perform. It has quite extensive responsibilities for social policy implementation, but it has little power of its own. There has since 1997 been a selective regional devolution of powers from Westminster to a Scottish Parliament, to National Assemblies for Wales and Northern Ireland respectively, and to a Greater London Assembly. This regional devolution has been quite limited, involving the transfer of relatively few powers (Parry 2003). At the sub-regional level there remains a network of County, District, City and Borough Councils; elected authorities with a range of tightly defined responsibilities in relation to education, housing and personal social service provision (Cochrane 2003). The UK's National Health Service is by and large centrally governed, but local control is delegated to a mixture of non-elected health authorities and trusts. Social security provision is entirely centrally administered, albeit through the locally situated offices of central government agencies.

As I have indicated, the UK is not necessarily typical, but the history of local government in the UK does serve to illustrate how a growth in centralized administrative power can change the context in which social policies are made and implemented. This is something that has occurred – to some extent – under all welfare regimes. In chapter 2, I explained how the making of capitalism and the development of social policies went hand in hand. Key to this was the centralization of administrative power. Central government took control over Poor Law administration. But the Poor Law still had to be locally administered and, paradoxically, the creation of local Poor Law Boards in the nineteenth century laid the foundations for the development of local government based on secular forms of state intervention; of the institutions through which, for example, state healthcare and child protection services would emerge; of the social casework techniques that provided the basis of modern social work practice. It was local government that organized the extension of municipal infrastructure – of sewage, water, gas and electricity supplies in the late nineteenth century. During the early part of the twentieth century, the size and scale of local government grew. In the period after the Second World War, however, elected local authorities lost their powers over health and social security provision, with the creation of the NHS and the modern social security system, albeit they did acquire substantial additional powers in relation to education, housing and the personal social services. Since the 1970s the functions of elected local authorities in the UK have been further curtailed and I shall discuss this further in chapter 9. In essence, however, local authorities are required increasingly to be enablers, rather than providers: to be the facilitators, commissioners and regulators of human service provision. While the role of elected local government in the UK has been diminishing, alternative modes of local governance have been emerging: modes of governance that, as we shall later see, are by no means unique to the UK.

From a Social Policy perspective, the local context can be the site at which centralized power is translated into action; at which – for good or ill – the state intrudes into everyday life. But it can also be the site at which there is a local democratic input to the policy-making process; at which the users of human services have their say. It is possible, in countries that permit local referenda on local taxes and services, that people may vote in favour of propositions that reduce social provision, as happened in California in the USA in 1978. In contrast, however, there is currently a lively debate about the ways in which local people in developing countries can and are being allowed effectively to participate in the control of local social spending – for example in Porto Alegre in Brazil (see Wainwright 2003).

The Nation State and the Policy Process

It is to the national policy-making process that we now turn. Unless we accept the 'strong' version of the globalization thesis that I discussed in chapter 3, we should acknowledge that the nation state, though its role may be changing, is not dead. Admittedly, the nation state is an entirely artificial construction, defined by relatively arbitrary territorial boundaries and often by the outcomes of war. The modern concept of the nation state emerged with the 1648 Treaty of Westphalia (that marked the end of Europe's Thirty Years War), by which it was agreed that in future sovereignty should vest in nations, and not in monarchs or emperors (e.g. Horsman and Marshall 1994). This concept has matured and endured. Nation states have always been subject to global economic influences, and, despite the growing power of transnational corporations and international governmental organizations, the nation state survives. It remains – for the time being at least – the basic building block of international relations. And it is still, in all but the poorest countries of the world, the key site for the processes by which social policies are decided (Hall and Midgley 2004).

One classic way of thinking about the policy making of nation states has been provided by systems analysis (Easton 1965). This highly formulaic approach looks upon any national policy-making process as a kind of black box that functions at the centre of a wider political environment and is subject to various inputs (demands for action or support for a particular approach) and produces various outputs (policy decisions and executive actions). The outputs generate a feedback loop that impacts on future inputs. Examining the inputs and outputs allows us to deduce what is going on inside the black box. More recent approaches, however, focus on the observable behaviour of political actors within the various policy networks that exist within and around governmental and policy-making processes (Rhodes 1997). More entertainingly, in a UK context, it should be admitted that the highly astute television comedy series, *Yes, Minister* and *Yes, Prime Minister* (Lynn and Jay 1984; 1986/7), have provided some telling insights into the inner workings of the Westminster policy machine.

There is huge diversity amongst the political systems of the world's nation states. Those that approximate to the liberal democratic ideal achieve a separation of constitutional powers in a variety of ways – some with presidential systems, some with surviving constitutional monarchies; some with written, but others with unwritten, constitutions; all with different voting systems and differently constituted legislatures. And we should not forget that, within the developing world, there are nations that in any event do not subscribe to the liberal democratic ideal (see chapter 3). This is not the place for a detailed discussion of the constitutional arrangements within which national policy-making processes may be situated, although it is important to consider some of the generic issues that currently face the welfare regimes of the developed world (see Hill 1997; Bochel and Bochel 2004):

Representation vs. *participation.* We have just seen that the principle of national sovereignty was established in the seventeenth century. In chapter 2, I presented the argument that the advent in the twentieth century of the capitalist welfare state entailed an extension of the principles of citizenship. The concept of citizenship is concerned with individual, not national, sovereignty. The modern concept is concerned with the way in which citizens can achieve the personal autonomy – as well as the social protection – that is necessary to human wellbeing. How far can a nation state square its own claims to sovereignty with those of its citizens? The liberal democratic compromise is a representative, rather than a participative, form of democracy (Held 1987). In liberal democracies we elect representatives to debate and to make policy on our behalf. Whether in principle this amounts to a form of popular sovereignty, or whether in practice sovereignty is thereby vested in the elected legislature, is a moot point. (In the UK the sovereign law-making powers of the monarch are delegated to Parliament, not the people, who, technically speaking, are still subjects, not citizens!) Are the representatives sitting on legislative bodies around the world – Parliaments, Assemblies, Senates, etc. – truly representative of, and accountable to, the people who periodically elect them? It may be argued that we need to establish a more participative form of democracy. Governments often pay lip service to participative principles – for example, through the promotion of consultation processes

– but often it is unrepresentative activists or self-appointed experts who participate, not ordinary people. Characteristically it is the poorest and most vulnerable citizens – those who most depend on human services – who have the least opportunity to participate in decision making (see Beresford and Turner 1997).

Executive power. We have seen that although elected legislatures may be responsible for passing the laws that give expression to social policies, it is the executive limb of government that puts policy into effect, or that initiates and oversees that process. Under presidential systems, such as that in the USA, the President is elected separately from the chambers of the legislature and it is s/he who appoints the other members of the executive. The executive therefore has its own power base and its own mandate. Under the kind of parliamentary system that there is in the UK, the executive (the Prime Minister and Cabinet) is drawn from the members of the legislature. The executive is uniquely placed to shape the agenda of the legislature and to control the policy-making process. In both scenarios there is a risk that constitutional checks and balances may be subverted in favour of the executive. The growing complexity of national governance in a global context – including the speed with which certain kinds of decision may need to be made – militates in favour of executive intervention and limits the extent to which the actions of the executive may be scrutinized.

Party politics. Representative democracy has spawned party political systems, which serve to structure the choices that are made available to the electorate. Because they cannot directly participate in the policy-making process, voters are presented with a choice between the manifestos of contending political parties. Each party presents voters with a fixed *table d'hôte* rather than an *à la carte* policy menu. Often, the contest is dominated by two main contenders: for example Conservative *vs.* Labour; Republican *vs.* Democrat; Christian Democrat *vs.* Social Democrat. Minor parties or independent candidates may play, at best, a minor role. The system may also have an inhibiting effect on debate within legislative chambers since elected members are likely to be bound by party loyalty or discipline to act in a certain way.

Voting systems. Associated with the issue of party politics is the question of how voting within a representative democracy may be organized. Though a variety of systems is possible, the fundamental distinction to be drawn is between majoritarian (or 'first-past-the-post') and proportional voting systems. English-speaking countries, broadly speaking, tend to favour majoritarian voting, at least for national elections, but some continental European countries have moved towards proportional voting. Majoritarian systems – which give victory in any particular constituency to the candidate(s) with the most votes – tend to favour two-party systems, so that over time policy may oscillate between right-wing and left-wing approaches, depending on the mood of the electorate. Proportional systems are fairer to minor political parties, since they make sure that parties are represented within the legislative chamber in proportion to the number of votes that they win. They result more often than majoritarian systems in inconclusive results and in coalition government. There is some evidence that though countries with proportional voting systems may be more stable in policy terms, this may mean that they are more path-dependent (see chapter 3) and less able to adapt to changing circumstances (Taylor-Gooby 2002).

In the realms of national policy making, the enduring mantra, attributed to Bill Clinton during his 1996 US presidential election campaign, is 'It's the economy, stupid'. Economic policy has always taken precedence over social policy. Commentators such as Alan Walker (1984) have argued that this need not be so, but as Kenneth Galbraith points out, politicians have good reason to court the votes of the 'contented majority' (1992). These are the voters who most benefit from national economic prosperity. For Social Policy, there are two important things to bear in mind. First, as we have seen, the contented majority is likely to be a major beneficiary of social provision. Second, societies purporting to be democratic, regardless of their government's political complexion, *ought* to be able to safeguard the wellbeing of marginalized minorities.

Regional Governance

Although I have already used the term 'regional' in connection with *sub*-national devolution, the term can also – confusingly – be used to refer to *supra*-national (but sub-global) bodies, such as the European Union (EU). There is a variety of such bodies – including, for example, the North American Free Trade Association (NAFTA), the Economic Commission for Latin America and the Caribbean (ECLAC), the Central European Free Trade Association (CEFTA), the Asia-Pacific Economic Co-operation Forum (APEC), the South Asian Association for Regional Co-operation Preferential Trade Arrangement (SAPTA), the Common Market for Eastern and Southern Africa (COMESA) – though, as is clear from their titles, some of these bodies are primarily focused on economic co-operation and terms of trade between the participating nations. However, the EU has gone further than most of the other regional associations in terms of developing a role beyond economic co-operation and trade. Insofar as it has significance for Social Policy, I shall briefly outline what this emerging tier of international governance entails (but see Geyer 2000; Hantrais 2003).

The EU began in 1957 as the European Economic Community, which was then composed of just six Western European states. The association has, by stages, both widened and deepened to become the EU. It now includes some 25 member states (including the UK) and is as much a political as an economic union. Specifically, it claims to embody an explicit 'social dimension' (CEC 1993). Initial limited co-operation on social policy matters focused on the harmonization of selected aspects of labour market regulation and social security, and the application of modest levels of structural funding to help improve the economic infrastructure of relatively disadvantaged sub-regions within the EU. There appears to have been a twofold impetus. On the one hand, there were fears amongst several member states of what was called 'social dumping'. This is the term used to describe what happens when a country cuts back on social protection for its workers in order to reduce wage costs and increase labour market flexibility and so achieve an unfair competitive advantage against its fellow EU members. The aim therefore was to get EU member states to accept broadly comparable levels of social protection. However, Jacques Delors, who served as head of the European Commission (the EU's executive) from 1985 to 1994, gave further impetus through his desire to expand *l'espace social* and to make the EU a positive influence in the advancement of social policy. The EU promulgated a Charter of Fundamental Social Rights in 1989. Extended versions of this were incorporated as Social Protocols to the 1992 and 1997 Maastricht and Amsterdam Treaties and it is intended, at the time of writing, that these should be consolidated into a proposed EU Constitution. Even if the Constitution were ratified, however, the rights so created would, arguably, be more symbolic than real, and would not be enforceable by individual citizens. The development of the social dimension has been quite late and relatively weak.

The EU's approach has been informed by the principle of 'subsidiarity'; the idea that responsibility for action should be devolved to the lowest possible tier or level of governance. To an extent this may be seen as a recipe for inertia. None the less, in certain key areas the EU has the power to pass or make regulations, directions, recommendations, resolutions or opinions. Of particular importance has been the use of directions in the area of equal treatment and health and safety at work, including the regulation of 'atypical' (e.g. part-time or casual) work and of working hours. Directions lay down objectives that member states must observe but leave states free to determine for themselves how they should legislate to achieve those objectives. These directions have had a significant impact in forcing changes in both employment law and aspects of social security legislation in the UK. Additionally, from 2000, a new 'Open Method of Co-ordination' (OMC) has been adopted in relation to the EU's Employment and Social Inclusion Strategies. The OMC requires member states to submit periodic National Action Plans, demonstrating the extent of their progress in relation to the specified objectives, and these Plans are then evaluated, reported upon and used to update the strategic objectives.

Though the influence upon the policy making of individual member states may be relatively indirect, for Social Policy, the EU is now providing an important forum for the analysis and discussion of policy development. It also offers interesting precedents or models that other regional bodies may in time follow.

Summary

This chapter has explored some of the political dimensions of Social Policy. It has outlined four main concerns:

- We cannot address issues of human wellbeing without addressing issues of power and, in particular, the political power that is entailed in the policy-making process. The chapter has discussed the particular way in which the power of modern capitalist states is legitimated; the different dimensions in which power can operate; and some competing interpretations of the functioning of the state.
- Social policies have to be implemented at the local level. The chapter has discussed the role of the administrators and professionals who deliver human services at 'street level', and the effects they can have in interpreting policy. It has also discussed the role of local government. Local government responsibilities and functions can be very different in different countries, but the chapter has illustrated some general issues associated with local governance. In particular, local government has remained critically important, even as administrative power has become more centralized.
- Most policy making still takes place at the level of the nation state. Nation states vary in terms of the way they conform or approximate to principles of democratic government, but the chapter has explored some general issues associated with the policy-making process and the nature of representative democracy. In particular, powerless minorities tend to be excluded from effective participation in the policy-making process, which is characteristically dominated by economic interests rather than social considerations.

- Finally, there is a potentially important tier of regional governance situated at a level between the nation state and the global institutions discussed in chapter 3. To illustrate this, the chapter has briefly explored the social policies of the EU.

7

What's the Trouble with Human Society?

Having fleetingly visited the economic and political dimensions of Social Policy in the last two chapters, in this chapter I shall outline elements of the subject's all-important social or sociological dimension. Social Policy has to contend with the complex and changing nature of human society. It must account for the conflicts that characterize human society, for its amazing adaptability and for the meanings that it brings to individual needs and experiences. Some sociologists have portrayed human society as if it resembled a perfectly functioning organism or machine; as a system that tends towards some natural or pre-set equilibrium. If this were so, there would be little need for Social Policy. A necessary part of Social Policy's job is to understand the troubles of human society. This should not imply that the function of social policies is simply to 'treat' or to 'fix' those troubles. Social policies are not things that are done to society, but by society. They are not visited upon society from the outside, but devised from within. Existing social policies are already integral to society and can sometimes be as much a part of society's troubles as a solution to them. Social Policy, as an academic subject, is concerned with how society succeeds or fails to promote human wellbeing.

I shall start by addressing the social diversity that stems from the fact that the humans who make up society are not all the same, and that difference may lead to disadvantage. Second, I shall consider how social conflicts over the general distribution of resources may elide with, or distract from, social conflicts over the recognition of particular needs or identities. Third, I shall discuss social inequality and social exclusion.

Finally, I shall explore the ways that society changes as the nature of the individual human life course changes.

Diversity and Difference

Though we are members of the same species, human beings are subject to biological differences. We are of different sexes and ages, we have different skin colours and physical characteristics, we start out with different genetically determined propensities, and in the course of our lives we are likely to experience different bodily drives, states of health and degrees of impairment. However, because we are social beings, these biological characteristics take on social meanings and significance. And it is with these 'socially constructed' differences that we are mainly concerned. I shall briefly discuss gender, 'race', age and disability as four socially constructed types of difference with considerable significance for Social Policy (see Dean 2003):

Gender. Approximately half the members of the human species are female and the other half male. Women have babies, men cannot. But the important difference between the sexes is not biological. It stems from a gendered division of labour by which it is characteristically women who care for children, hearth and home, while men have been free to hunt and gather; to engage in economic production and political governance. We saw in chapter 2 how women have in the past been excluded from masculine assumptions about the nature of citizenship. As H. G. Wells' fictional Miss Miniver rightly put it, 'It's our very importance that degrades us [women]. While we were minding the children they [the men] stole our rights and liberties' (1909: ch. 2). It isn't simply that women tend to mind the children. It has been calculated that around two thirds of all the world's work is performed by women (e.g. UNDP 2001), including subsistence farming in many developing countries, and to an ever greater extent in the formal labour markets of the developed world. But women's work tends systematically to be undervalued. Women are at greater risk of poverty than men because they tend to be dependent within their families or households. Additionally, when they do have access to independent income from the labour market, they cannot necessarily do so on the same terms (or at the same pay-rates) as men. The capitalist welfare state has, none the less, been important for women, since it has succeeded in redistributing resources from men to women (Falkingham and Hills 1995). But in a variety of ways it has also tended to reinforce deep-rooted assumptions about women's dependency on men and to leave women relatively disadvantaged – in relation to pensions, for example. And though women have been especially important to the development of social policies – as nurses, teachers and social workers, for example – they have been systematically under-represented in the processes of human service management and social policy making (Lewis 2003; Pascall 1997)

'Race'. Although it is phenotypically diverse, there is only one human species. The concept of 'race', it is now generally accepted, is a scientific misnomer. It is the social processes of migration and settlement, the competition and co-operation between different social groups and the building of nations and empires that have divided the human species into ethnically or culturally distinctive groups. It is through the relations of power and subordination between those groups that the differences between them become 'racialized': a term that appears first to have been used by Franz Fanon (1967) to capture the sense in which colonial oppression depended on an ideologically shaped awareness of difference. 'Race' is a myth (which is why I place the word in inverted commas), but *racism* is a very real phenomenon. Racism is more than the fear of 'otherness', or a mistrust of cultural difference. It informs oppressive social practices and institutions. It was inherent to the horrors of slavery in the pre-capitalist era and colonial exploitation in the era of capitalist imperialism. It provides a context for the systemic marginalization of many developing nations from global markets and the international economy. It explains the 'ethnic penalty' to which indigenous and diasporic minority ethnic groups within the developed world may be subject. In the UK, for example, an official government report has recently conceded that 'in comparison to their representation in the population, people from minority ethnic communities are more likely than others to live in poor areas; be poor; be unemployed, compared with white people with similar qualifications; suffer ill health and live in overcrowded and unpopular housing. They also experience widespread racial harassment and racial crime and are over-represented in the criminal justice system, from stop and search to prison.' (SEU 2000: ch.2; and see Ahmad and Craig 2003).

Age. After we are born, we are all expected to grow up, and to grow old. And yet 'young' and 'old' are relative terms. Their meaning and consequences are socially defined. In parts of the developing world and, in the past, throughout the developed world, children are or were expected to work from an early age and to continue working until as adults they died or were too frail to work. Associated with the process of capitalist development have been social policies that reflect changing assumptions about childhood and old age. Children are protected from labour market exploitation and sent to school. Older people are enabled to withdraw from the labour market after a certain age, notwithstanding that people are living longer and healthier lives. We have invented a particular understanding of 'youth' (as a potentially problematic stage of transition between childhood and adulthood) and 'retirement' (as a potentially burdensome stage of transition between active adulthood and death). Insofar as they are not regarded as fully adult workers or citizens, young people and old people may suffer disadvantage. In countries like the UK, young people characteristically have fewer rights and are subject to more restrictions than adults and yet, in the process of the transitions they must undergo, they are demonstrably vulnerable to poverty and, as they approach adulthood, homelessness and unemployment (Coles 2003). Older people are similarly vulnerable to discrimination, poverty and exclusion from many aspects of workplace, community and everyday life (Walker and Maltby 2003).

Disability. Some of us are born with genetic impairments, others will in the course of our lives suffer illness, injury or degenerative conditions that will limit our functioning. Insofar as people with physical, mental or learning impairments are defined as 'disabled', the question this begs is whether it is their impairments that disable them, or society. Is it biology that diminishes their capacity fully to function as human beings, or society's failure to accommodate difference? As recently as the beginning of the twentieth century in countries such as the UK, some disabled people were regarded as a threat to the purity of the national 'stock' and were segregated from 'normal' people in special institutions. Later in the century, attitudes changed. Disability was generally regarded as a personal tragedy for those concerned and the emphasis, when appropriate, was on medical intervention and rehabilitation. In this way disabled people were, and often still are, construed as a burden on society, rather than as people whom society tends unjustly to exclude from participation. The wellbeing of disabled people is constrained by the absence or shortage of resources and facilities appropriate to their particular needs; by discrimination that keeps them out of education and jobs; by the characteristics of the built environment that restrict their mobility and ability to participate. Even in countries such as the UK, with benefits and services for disabled people, households that include disabled adults or children are at demonstrably greater risk of poverty than those households that don't (Oliver 2003).

There are conflicting views as to how to address the disadvantage that may result from difference. Capitalist welfare states have classically adopted a compensatory social welfare approach. Directly or indirectly, women have been accorded benefits and services that support them in their role as mothers. Initiatives have been taken, especially in the context of urban regeneration policy, to assist minority ethnic groups better to integrate with the majority communities among which they live. Facilities, such as recreation and advice services, have been developed for young people, and pensions policies make a major contribution to provision for older people. Compensatory benefits schemes and specialist domiciliary and residential care services have been developed for disabled people. An alternative approach – that may, none the less, operate in parallel with a compensatory social welfare approach – is a liberal equal opportunities approach. Anti-discrimination legislation and equal opportunities policies have been promoted in several developed countries, including the UK, to try and prevent discrimination against women, against members of minority ethnic groups, against older (but not necessarily younger) people and against disabled people. Such legislation is still in the process of being developed, but its aim is to ensure equal treatment at work, in education and in access to goods and services. The intention is to remove barriers to social and economic participation.

Broadly speaking, the compensatory approach aims to achieve a society that is humane and solidaristic: the equal opportunities approach, one that is tolerant and fair. However, both approaches have their critics. Compensatory approaches tend to perpetuate and consolidate rather than confront the implications of difference. They work from the implicit premise that difference is to be understood in relation to the norm of the white, working-age, able-bodied male. It is a premise that neglects the extent to which masculinity, 'majority' ethnicities and our understanding of life-course stages and of 'ability' are of themselves socially constructed and therefore inherently problematic. Equal opportunities approaches can fail to address the fundamental causes of disadvantage and underlying relations of power. They work from the implicit premise that it is discriminatory attitudes and prejudices that are the problem. It is a premise that neglects the extent to which attitudes are no more and no less than reflections or consequences of the institutional processes by which differences are socially constituted.

Feminist critics of the welfare state, therefore, are concerned that it does not combat the fundamentally patriarchal nature of society; compensatory approaches tend to lock women into dependency on men; equal opportunities approaches tend to force women to compete with men on men's terms. Anti-racist critics of the welfare state are concerned that it does not go far enough in combating racism: compensatory approaches result, at best, in a superficial form of multiculturalism that both trivializes and reifies ethnic differences; equal opportunities approaches may promote tactical forms of compliance that leave underlying institutional racism untouched. Similarly, so far as both young and old people are concerned, it may be argued that compensatory approaches are actually implicated in the process that makes age a problem; while equal opportunities approaches – so far as they exist – are of limited effect. Finally, the disability rights and independent living movements insist that compensatory social welfare approaches effectively deny that it is society that is to blame for the disadvantage that disabled people experience; while equal opportunities approaches, as presently conceived, do not go far enough in allowing disabled people that degree of autonomy and control over their own lives that is necessary for human wellbeing.

These radical critiques of the capitalist welfare state raise fundamental questions about the role of social policy within society.

Class and Identity

To understand this, we need to go back for a moment to the discussion in chapter 2 about citizenship and the welfare state. When he claimed that the development within capitalist society of social rights of citizenship would be a 'civilizing' force, T. H. Marshall (1950) was arguing that the welfare state would heal or ameliorate the old class conflicts that had characterized capitalism. The politics of the mid-twentieth century were based on class. Disadvantage was associated primarily with class difference. Sociology has several competing theories of class which we do not have the space to explore (see Abercrombie 2004). Essentially, however, all these theories are concerned to explain processes of social change in terms of evolving conflicts between economically defined social groups or classes. The welfare state can be understood, in part, as a concession that was wrung by the working class from the capitalist class (e.g. Bottomore 1992). Class politics was the struggle over the distribution of resources. It still clearly makes sense to draw a distinction between the interests of capital and the interests of labour and how these are reflected in social policies. But these days it doesn't necessarily make sense to think of capitalist society as being divided between 'the bosses' and 'the workers'.

So, whatever happened to class? First, it got more complicated. It is still possible to divide society up conceptually into different groups according to people's occupations on the premise that their occupations will reflect their economic or class interests. In the mid-twentieth century, in countries such as the UK, the most conspicuous cleavage in society was not (and never had been) between a tiny minority of capitalist 'bosses' and a mass of 'workers', but between a middle class, composed of non-manual workers, and a working class, composed of manual workers. Since then the middle class has expanded and fragmented. A relatively small group of powerful managers and professionals now constitute what is sometimes called a service class, with interests closely allied to capital, while growing numbers of routine non-manual workers have effectively been 'proletarianized' (Braverman 1974). Meanwhile, the effect of new technologies and of globalization has been to shrink the traditional manual working class and to accentuate a long-standing division between a highly skilled elite on the one hand and the routinely skilled or unskilled on the other. Another sociologist, Gordon Marshall (1997), has recently demonstrated that, despite changes in the occupational structure, class still matters. Class divisions directly correlate in contemporary capitalist societies with the unequal distribution of life chances.

The second thing that has happened to class, as a concept, is that it has fallen out of favour. The radical critiques that I outline above, particularly the feminist critique, have drawn attention to the ways in which class analysis and the old class politics tend to marginalize other kinds of social difference, such as gender, 'race', age and disability. Given that society itself is changing – not least because of the welfare state – these critiques suggest it is time to move on. In place of a politics of class, we need a new politics of identity. Instead of demanding a redistribution of resources to meet universal human needs, we should be demanding the proper recognition of social differences and provision to meet particular needs (Fraser and Honneth 2003). For my own part, I shall argue in chapter 10 that we need both kinds of politics. For now, however, I wish to focus on what is meant by 'social identity'.

It is, in part, through our differences from other people that we define our own identities. Our social identity is defined by gender, ethnicity and age and, for some, disability. Identity may also be defined – quite critically – by factors, such as sexuality and religion, that we do not have space here to discuss. And it should not be forgotten that class can itself be a source of identity. David Taylor (1998) has defined all these as 'categorical' identities. We are each of us unique as human beings. Our identity has several overlapping sources and is constituted as the sum of several categorical identities. A politics of identity celebrates the sources of our identities and argues for the recognition of the particular needs of particular people. On the face of it, a politics of identity favours selective as opposed to universal principles of distribution (see chapter 5).

However, Taylor has suggested there is another kind of identity, which he calls 'ontological' identity. Ontological identity stems from our sense of 'self'; from the integrity and autonomy of our person; from the coherence and unity of our being. We might argue that it is the essential and universal element of human wellbeing. The problem for Social Policy is how to reconcile the unique identities that human society bestows with the essential nature of our common humanity; or more simply, how to square particular claims with universal needs. This is something that all students of Social Policy must ponder – not as an interesting philosophical question, but as an issue of immense importance in the context of societies that are systemically unequal and exclusive.

Inequality and Exclusion

While we may celebrate aspects of the diversity of human society, we would not necessarily wish to celebrate social inequality. We have seen that socially constructed difference may result in social disadvantage. It may heighten people's vulnerability to poverty, a concept I touched upon in chapter 4 when discussing income maintenance. One way of thinking about poverty is as 'the unacceptable face of inequality' (Alcock 1993: 255).

However one defines the point at which social inequality becomes unacceptable, it may be seen that the extent of inequality in the world has generally been increasing, both between and within countries. In the course of the twentieth century, as living standards rose, absolute poverty around the world appeared to decrease. But social inequality increased (Bourguignon and Morrisson 2002). Between 1960 and the mid-1990s, the ratio between the share of income held by the richest fifth of the world's population to that held by the world's poorest fifth more than doubled from 30 : 1 to 78 : 1 (UNDP 1997: 9). In the UK during roughly the same period, the income share of the richest tenth of the population rose from 22 per cent to 25 per cent, while that of the poorest tenth fell from 4.2 per cent to 3 per cent (Goodman and Webb 1994: 66). Since then, the share of the poorest tenth has stayed much the same, but the share of the richest tenth has risen further to 28 per cent (Hills 2004: 23). As the rich get richer, the poor get relatively poorer, not only globally, but even within many of those developed nations that have established welfare states. It had been assumed that the welfare state would abolish poverty and contain inequality but in the UK, sociologists such as Peter Townsend (1979) demonstrated that this did not happen. During the 1980s, Margaret Thatcher's government denied the existence of poverty and asserted, in effect, that increasing inequality was quite acceptable (Moore 1989).

It was at this time that discussion about poverty and social inequality subsided. In its place, from continental Europe came the concept of social exclusion, and from the USA came the concept of 'underclass'. Social exclusion is the more important concept, because it has been widely adopted in various parts of the world (including, under Tony Blair's government, in the UK). The strength of the concept is that it is multidimensional (see Burchardt et al. 2002). It encompasses the idea that there are many factors – to do with income, resources and lifestyles, access to goods and services, participation in employment and civic life, engagement with friends and relatives – that all bear upon the extent to which people are 'included' in society. It is a concept that may be used to describe the dynamics of the processes by which people, at particular points in their lives and for particular reasons, may become distanced or removed from mainstream social activities. It can capture the complexity of the processes by which, for some individuals or social groups, multiple causes of exclusion may intersect and have catastrophic consequences. The potential weakness of the concept is that it is often interpreted in ways that focus on the failures of individuals or the communities in which they live, rather than on failures of the economic and social structures that may constrain the opportunities that are available to them (Levitas 1998). Authoritarian policy recipes for combating social exclusion may ignore the economic causes of social inequality and the deeper structural failures of society. They seek instead to change the behaviour of those – such as the long-term unemployed, young offenders, lone parents, rough sleepers – who are labelled as excluded.

The concept of underclass, because it was similarly authoritarian in its implications, generated considerable controversy when it began to be applied by commentators such as Charles Murray (1990). Murray has claimed that societies such as the USA and the UK are threatened by the emergence of a self-perpetuating and morally corrosive social class that is detached from mainstream social values. Three factors are contributing to the growth of this underclass: rising crime rates; rising numbers of children born outside marriage (especially to young women); rising levels of disengagement from the labour market (especially among young men). The solution, it is supposed, is a zero-tolerance approach to crime, but also to curtail the welfare state. State 'welfare' provision (particularly the provision of benefits to lone parents and the unemployed) undermines the incentives to marriage, employment and responsibility; it fosters a 'dependency culture'. Critics argue that no case can be made for the existence of a permanent underclass in any structural sense, and that there is little or no evidence – for example amongst long-term social security recipients – of a distinctive dependency culture (e.g. Dean and Taylor-Gooby 1992).

Debates about social exclusion and the underclass concept have focused on the processes by which some people may be pulled or pushed to the margins of society. The rich can be as excluded from society as ɔor, especially if they choose to isolate themselves in affluent gated ɦunities, as they do in many parts of the world. The debates, though may sometimes have distracted us from discussing social inequality, have actually been about the consequences and manifestations of inequality in a changing social context.

Social Change and the Life Course

And it is to change that we now turn. We have discussed the economic changes that shape society (see chapters 2 and 3) but there have been other very basic and far-reaching changes whose effects so far as Social Policy is concerned are, in some respects, even more immediate. Here we are concerned with two kinds of social or demographic change: changes in the composition of the population; and changes in household formation.

Countries that experience the process of capitalist economic development characteristically undergo not only the kind of epidemiological transition mentioned in chapter 4 but also a fundamental demographic transition. The nature of that transition can be summed up in the simple phrase: 'fewer babies, longer lives' (Ermisch 1990). As societies become more affluent, fertility or birth rates tend to decline while average life expectancy tends to increase. In the UK, for example, from the turn of the twentieth century to the turn of the twenty-first, fertility rates more than halved from an average of 3.5 to 1.6 births per woman; average life expectancy at birth increased from around 50 years to 78 years (see Halsey 1988; UNDP 2003). In developing countries, by contrast, fertility rates remain much higher and life expectancy much lower. In Sierra Leone, for example, the estimated fertility rate is currently 6.5 births per woman and average life expectancy is just 34 years. The rise in life expectancy can easily be understood as the consequence of rising living standards and improved health provision. The decline in fertility stems not only from improvements in contraceptive technologies but also from changing social habits and expectations. In poor countries, such as Sierra Leone, with little or no social provision, it makes sense for people to have several children in the hope that some of their offspring will survive long enough to be able to provide for their parents when they grow old.

Demographic transition in the developed world is a mixed blessing. On the one hand, declining fertility curtails population growth, which is good news for environmental sustainability. However, a society in which women have on average fewer than two babies each in the course of their lives will, self-evidently, fail to reproduce itself over time. That the population will eventually contract, is not necessarily a problem. But the changing age profile of the population may well be. Just as people in poor countries expect their offspring to care for them in their old age, then so must the populations of rich countries, albeit the mechanisms by which that care is organized are different. In most developed countries, it is in practice the current generation of working age adults who are paying through their taxes and social security contributions for the state pensions, health and social care provision that are received by the current generation of older people. As we have fewer babies, this eventually feeds through into smaller generations of working age adults. As we live longer, each generation of older people grows larger. As a result, it has been suggested, some developed countries are now confronting a 'demographic time-bomb' (NEDO 1989) because the working age population will no longer be able to afford the social costs of the pensioner population.

The threat posed by population ageing is probably overstated (e.g. Hills 2004: ch. 10). Fewer babies will mean smaller cohorts of school pupils and savings on state education. Rising productivity and wages will make it possible for a smaller workforce to pay more in taxes. Though we live longer, more of us remain healthy and active in old age and the length of time during which we may require intensive health or social care will not necessarily be that much longer than in the past. In many developed countries, an increasing proportion of the cost of pensions is met through occupational and private pension schemes that have already been paid for (though the value of accrued pension funds may be jeopardized by financial malpractice and falling stock prices). The issue is more serious for some countries than for others. The general question for Social Policy, however, has to do with the social sustainability of human populations. If continual economic development leads to people having fewer babies, then we may have to accept that as individuals we shall each have to bear a higher proportionate share of social costs. If we continue to enjoy ever-longer lives, then we may have to accept that we shall have to work and to earn for longer.

Associated with demographic transition are long-term changes in the way that families and households are formed. These are illustrated in box 7.1. This fluidity of family types and diversity of household forms poses several questions for Social Policy. The first of these relates to housing provision and the demand for greater numbers of smaller units of accommodation. Second, there is a range of issues concerning the extent to which social policies may affect people's freedom to move in and out of relationships, or to choose with whom they should live. In particular, we have already seen that the prevalence of lone parenthood in developed countries has provoked debate about the role of the state,

Box 7.1 Fluid families

- Generally in developed countries, but particularly in the UK, there has in recent decades been a decline in first marriage rates, a rise in cohabitation (often as a precursor to marriage), a rise in divorce rates and an increase in the incidence of lone parenthood, but a rise also in the incidence of remarriage, reconstituted families and step-families (Pahl 2003).
- These changes, together with the changes in fertility that have been explained in this chapter, are associated with a trend towards smaller households and family sizes. In particular, there has been an increase in single-person households and in people living alone. In part, this is associated with changing social attitudes towards intimate relationships (Abercrombie 2004).
- However, economic prosperity and social policies have facilitated some of these changes. In increasingly affluent societies young people are better able to leave the parental home to live independently without establishing a family of their own. At the other end of the age scale, the availability of state pensions has made it possible for old people to continue to live independently and often alone, when in the past they might otherwise have had to live with their adult offspring (Finch 1989).
- Similarly, social assistance arrangements have made it possible for women who have been subject to violent and abusive relationships to leave their husbands or partners, and to maintain themselves and their children independently as lone parents.

and questions as to whether social policies should encourage or deter lone parenthood. Social assistance and 'workfare' regimes (see chapter 4) may be used to place pressure on lone parents to re-partner or to find employment. Child support systems that force absent parents to pay maintenance for their children may be used to place pressure on families to stay together (e.g. Bradshaw 2003). We might ask, however, whether and why lone parenthood is a problem? In the UK, for example, most lone parents (90 per cent) are women and, of these, most have previously been married or in a cohabiting relationship. The proportion who have never lived with their children's father is relatively small. What is more, lone parenthood tends to be a temporary status: most lone parents do re-partner. It is simply that the nature of the family as a social institution is changing, as indeed it has changed throughout history (see Gittens 1993).

I have already discussed the concept of social identity. Within the ordinary life course people acquire, or are socially assigned, a succession of categorical identities: as children, as young people, as workers, as parents, as pensioners. They may move in and out of different households and different intimate relationships, and each transition not only qualifies their categorical identity but may also profoundly affect their ontological identity. Throughout the life course, Social Policy is relevant to understanding whether identity confers wellbeing, and the extent to which, within their social context, people's lives have integrity.

Summary

This chapter has explored some of the sociological dimensions of Social Policy. It has outlined four main concerns:

- The diversity of human beings and the meanings society attaches to the differences between them. Specifically, the chapter has addressed differences based on gender, 'race', age and disability. In each instance it has illustrated how difference is associated with disadvantage – for women, for the members of minority ethnic groups, for young and old people, and for disabled people. It has discussed how social policies may seek to compensate for such disadvantages, or to promote equal opportunities; but also how feminist, anti-racist, senior citizens' and disabled people's movements challenge the ways in which existing forms of welfare state provision may in some respects perpetuate social disadvantage.
- The tension between an understanding of society based on class analysis and an understanding based on theories of social identity. The chapter has outlined how one sociological interpretation sees the capitalist welfare state as a partial victory in a struggle over the social distribution of resources; but also how emergent critical analyses prioritize struggles to achieve recognition of diverse identities and provision for specific needs. It has discussed how Social Policy must reconcile these ostensibly conflicting approaches in order to understand how it may be possible to meet both universal needs and particular claims.
- The problems of social inequality and social exclusion. The chapter has explained that the extent of inequality is increasing in spite of the development of welfare states but, instead of focusing on inequality, recent debate has focused on concepts such as social exclusion and underclass. The former may be used to capture the dynamic and multidimensional nature of social disadvantage, but it shares with the

latter a tendency to attribute disadvantage to individual behaviour rather than structural constraints.

- Social and demographic change and the dynamic nature of the human life course. The chapter has outlined the nature and consequences of the demographic transition and population ageing that characteristically accompanies the process of capitalist economic development, and the social changes currently affecting the formation and composition of families and households, including the emergence of the lone-parent family form. It reflects on the changing nature of the identities and relationships that people experience in the course of their lives and the relevance of this for Social Policy.

8

Can Social Policy Solve Social Problems?

The principal focus of this book has been on the promotion of human wellbeing, not the solving of social problems. If it were to focus *only* on social problems Social Policy might well become a rather dismal subject. This is why, at the beginning of the last chapter, I made the point that the function of Social Policy is not restricted to treating or fixing the troubles of human society. But it remains the case that Social Policy, as a subject, is crucially relevant to solving social problems and to understanding the double-edged role that prevailing social policies can sometimes play in relation to social problems.

I like to think that Social Policy's approach to problem solving is akin to that, not of a social engineer, so much as a social architect. Social policy solutions should aim not to manipulate people, but to buttress those elements of social structure that will support human wellbeing and counteract those that undermine it. Social problems may be understood as features of the social fabric that undermine human wellbeing. In this chapter I shall firstly explore what we understand social problems to be. I shall then discuss the important idea that it is through rights to social justice that we can right the wrongs of society before moving on to consider the implications of competing approaches to the explanation of social problems. Finally, I shall briefly discuss some issues relating to criminal justice policy which, though it has not always been associated with Social Policy, is of increasing relevance to debates about social problem solving.

The (De-)construction of Social Problems

In chapter 7, I explained how some of the differences between people are not necessarily 'natural', but 'socially constructed'. Our sense of who we are is determined by the historical and social context in which we live out our lives. Similarly, the significance of the problems that we experience in life is constructed by our social context. An emerging tradition in the social sciences – sometimes called post-structuralism (e.g. Sarup 1993) – aims through a process it calls *de*construction to demystify the way that meaning is constructed. Rather less abstractly than this, we saw in chapter 6 how important it is to understand how the political agenda is shaped. Part of the process of deconstructing a social problem involves an analysis of the role of interest groups, politicians, the press and the broadcasting media in identifying and defining issues. In his celebrated analysis of 1960s' youth culture, Stan Cohen (1980) demonstrated how society periodically contrives to turn particular social groups into 'folk devils' and to turn particular social concerns into 'moral panics'.

Without necessarily attaching particular theoretical labels to the process, Social Policy's practical analytical approach has been 'deconstructing' social problems for years (Manning 1985; May et al. 2001). One of Social Policy's great strengths has been its capacity for the critical analysis of social problems; for showing how problems have arisen; for re-interpreting them in their wider social context; and for commenting, for example, on the ambiguity of current policy approaches. There are any number of examples from which I might choose, but I shall illustrate what I mean using just four:

Lone parenthood. We touched on the subject of lone parenthood in the last chapter. The dramatic rise in the numbers of lone parents during the last part of the twentieth century in countries such as the UK is often identified as a 'social problem'. As we have seen, it was a phenomenon driven by social change and, in particular, a long-term shift in the nature of family relationships. Lone parenthood itself is not new, however. Widowhood had been common enough in the past, but increasing longevity means that marriages and relationships have to last longer. Women are more likely to experience lone parenthood as a result of separation or divorce than as a result of the death of a partner. More fundamental, perhaps, have been the changes by which 'sex has become separated from marriage and marriage from parenthood' (Lewis 2001: 37). As a manifestation of this secular trend, the lone parent began in the 1980s to acquire symbolic folk devil status.

She was regarded as a portent of the demise of the traditional family. Former Prime Minister Margaret Thatcher reflected, after leaving office, that 'we could only get to the roots of crime and much else besides by concentrating on strengthening the traditional family' (1995: 628). Lone parents were demonized by certain conservative politicians and in the right-wing press. They were condemned for sponging from the state if they relied on social assistance but for letting their children run out of control if they went to work. It is clear that lone parents remain especially vulnerable to poverty, and there is contentious evidence that children growing up in lone-parent households may fare worse in later life than children from two-parent households. An ambiguous raft of policy changes and developments has ensued, some intended to provide incentives for parents to stay together, but others to promote lone parents' capacity for independence from the state.

Homelessness. We saw in chapter 4 that homelessness, like lone parenthood, is hardly new. It has been a policy issue for centuries. But, taking the UK as our example, homelessness was reconstituted as a particular kind of social problem in the last part of the twentieth century (Liddiard 2001). The initial impetus came in this instance not from moral conservatism (as happened with lone parenthood) but from liberal social concern. In 1966 an iconic television docudrama by Ken Loach, *Cathy Come Home*, shocked the British public into awareness of the treatment suffered by homeless families. In spite of the UK's considerable investment in public housing during the post-Second World War period, emergency provision for homeless people had remained a residual local government responsibility. Homeless families were treated by and large much as they had been under the Poor Law. Mothers and children were put into forbidding hostels, and fathers left to fend for themselves. The families were seldom properly supported or rehoused, and were often allowed to disintegrate. In the wake of *Cathy Come Home*, a national campaign led by the charity Shelter resulted in the 1970s in new legislation that for the first time placed a duty on local housing authorities to house homeless families with children. That duty – which was in any event conditional upon families not having made themselves intentionally homeless – has since been qualified in a variety of different ways. The legislation was enough, nevertheless, to salve the public conscience so far as family homelessness was concerned. More recently, however, a different kind of moral panic has been generated, this time by politicians and the media, and addressed not to family homelessness but to street homelessness and the incidence of rough sleeping on the streets of the UK. This panic has justified the use of a 'zero-tolerance' approach to street homelessness and measures to force homeless single people out of sight and into hostel accommodation.

Domestic violence. Once again, though the term 'domestic violence' may be relatively new, the abuse of women by their partners is by no means a recent phenomenon. However, rather like homelessness, it is an issue that managed to force its way onto the public agenda in the 1970s (see Radford 2001). The impetus in the UK came in this instance from the publicity that surrounded the work of Erin Pizzey, who founded the first of an independent national network of women's refuges. Without doubt, the rise of feminism contributed to changing attitudes, but it was vociferous campaigning by and on behalf of the survivors of domestic violence that succeeded in raising awareness. As a result, legislation was introduced in the 1970s to provide improved protection for those experiencing or at risk of domestic violence; improvements were made in the 1980s and '90s to police procedures for investigating incidents of domestic violence; and, more recently, there have been government-sponsored attempts to promote local multi-agency initiatives to support women experiencing domestic violence. None the less, the evidence suggests a great deal of domestic violence continues to go undetected and there remains a sense in which domestic violence is regarded 'as a women's issue, rather than as an issue for men' (Radford 2001: 80). Despite the relatively high profile achieved for the issue, effective policy responses have tended to focus on assisting women to escape from violence, rather than confronting the behaviour of men.

Drug abuse. Drugs have been used by human beings throughout history. The use of certain kinds of drug, such as alcohol, is widespread and in many countries culturally acceptable. However, the consumption of drugs that are not culturally acceptable is socially constituted not as 'use', but 'abuse' or 'misuse' (see Gould 2001). All drugs are potentially dangerous, and yet they tend only to become a cause of moral panic when they are perceived to be culturally 'alien'. The processes of globalization described in chapter 3 have served to extend the trade in all sorts of drugs. Throughout the twentieth century, in countries such as the USA and the UK, drugs, such as opiates and hallucinogens, have tended to be regarded as illicit when they have been associated with the potentially corrupting habits of immigrant minorities or foreigners. There have been recurrent panics about the threat they pose to the innocent. Experts disagree about the definition and meaning of concepts such as 'addiction' and 'dependency', but what is clear is that there is a distinction to be drawn between casual and recreational forms of illicit drug use (however risky) and the profoundly problematic forms of drug use that are associated with socially marginalized groups and highly vulnerable individuals (such as the street homeless and people with mental health problems). That association is made more complicated and less transparent by the fact that trading and possessing the drugs in question is illegal. The danger is that the drugs problem can be offered up as 'a reason for many of the problems that politicians cannot or will not deal with' (Gould 2001: 224). Policy in the developed world tends to embrace a contradictory mixture of, on the one hand, education and harm reduction strategies that aim to discourage drug use and minimize the risks faced by drug users and, on the other, policies that further criminalize particular kinds of drug use and seek to punish rather than to treat those whose drug use has become problematic.

Even if they had not been cast as 'social problems', lone parenthood, homelessness, domestic violence and drug abuse are all, or can all be, catastrophically problematic for those who experience them. But it is the way in which they have come to be constituted as social problems that seems to result in policy approaches that are ambiguous or even contradictory. And it is this that Social Policy, as a subject, must try and understand.

The Righting of Wrongs

If Social Policy must struggle to understand what's wrong with society and with existing policies, it must also consider the various ways in which these may be put right. The various problems faced by lone parents, homeless people, by those who experience domestic violence and by those engaging in harmful forms of drug use may be understood as social injustices; as the violation of a person's rights, for example, to social security, freely chosen work, shelter, physical safety and effective healthcare intervention.

As should be clear from the discussion of citizenship in chapter 2, the concept of 'rights' is central to Social Policy (see Dean 2002). But where do our rights come from? There is a view that there are certain inherent and inalienable rights that all human beings possess; rights that are divinely or naturally bestowed and which we may discover. The alternative view is that the only rights that we enjoy are those that human societies define for themselves. These may be the kind of rights that are conceded or imposed from above by those in power, or those that are demanded or seized from below by the people. Sociological accounts of citizenship (e.g. Turner 1990) contend that our rights have indeed been socially constructed, and that they are a mixture of what lawyers would call 'black letter rights' that are written down and are justiciable before the courts, and 'moral rights' or 'manifesto rights' that are the basis of policy debates and struggles to promote human wellbeing. We have already seen that according to T. H. Marshall (1950) citizenship rights have come to include civil and political rights on the one hand and social rights on the other. Civil and political rights are associated mainly with the formal protection of individual freedoms; in particular, the freedom of the property-owning subject from undue interference by strangers, neighbours or the state itself. Social rights, however, are concerned with substantive social protection, not formal legal protection; they are often positively framed in terms of rights *to* the resources we need for wellbeing, as well as in terms of freedom *from* harm.

In 1948 the newly created United Nations (UN) proclaimed the Universal Declaration of Human Rights (UDHR). The concept of Human Rights was presented as if it was a timeless or self-evident doctrine, but the rights propounded by the UDHR were clearly premised on socially constructed liberal-democratic notions of citizenship. The UDHR drew essentially the same distinction as T. H. Marshall between civil and political rights on the one hand and what were defined as economic, social and cultural rights on the other. However, these two classes of rights were subsequently put into effect using separate international covenants under which economic, social and cultural rights were subject to a wholly ineffectual monitoring and enforcement regime. Where regional bodies have adopted the principles of the UDHR, the same thing has tended to happen. For example, the Council of Europe's Convention on Human Rights, which encompasses mainly civil and political rights, created the European Court of Human Rights. But its sister document, the European Social Charter, containing economic, social and cultural rights, created only a committee-based monitoring mechanism. None the less, selected elements of the European Social Charter are incorporated in the Charter of Fundamental Rights of the European Union (see chapter 6). Additionally, UN agencies are currently seeking to make Human Rights principles central to the eradication of world poverty (OHCHR 2002).

Because social rights have tended hitherto to be a poor relation to civil and political rights, the language of rights has not always served Social Policy well. From a neo-liberal perspective, the only rights that matter are those that protect the life, liberty and property of the individual subject. From a neo-Marxist perspective, rights are a dangerous fiction that tends to obscure the fundamentally oppressive nature of the relations between capital and labour and between the capitalist state and the individual subject. But the language of rights does provide a powerful medium through which to define human needs and to frame claims to the resources required for human wellbeing. Also, where social policies – through constitutional or legislative instruments – do succeed in creating rights to human services, they may also secure the means to enforce or to extend the interpretation of such rights through the courts or through other mechanisms of redress. The welfare rights movement has had an important part to play in social policy development, particularly in the English-speaking world (Schiengold 1974; Prosser 1983).

Within Social Policy there are those who strongly advocate a rights-based approach, both at a national and the global level. Despite its attractions, critics of the rights-based approach claim that it can easily end up neglecting the causes of the problems it seeks to address. By focusing on individual rights it may, on the one hand, leave individual responsibilities out of account (Roche 1992). It may, on the other, leave the social and structural determinants of individual problems untouched (Piven and Cloward 1977). In other words, a rights approach may not bother to ask who is to blame for social problems.

Blaming the Victim

It is to this question that I now turn. I am not merely concerned with how social problems arrive on the political agenda but with how they are to be analysed and interpreted. William Ryan (1971; 1977) has suggested that the dominant approach in the late twentieth century, particularly in the USA, has been to 'blame the victim'. The explanation of social problems is to be found in the behaviour of those affected by the problem. So, for example, many lone parents could have avoided their difficulties had they not chosen to have children, or if they had not unnecessarily left their partners. Homeless people could have avoided their predicament had they chosen to continue to live with their families until they were properly self-sufficient, or if they had paid their rent or mortgage instalments on time. Women who have suffered domestic violence might have avoided it if they had exited from a dangerous relationship before it became violent. Drug abusers could have avoided their addiction had they been less weak or irresponsible. Ryan himself condemned this approach, preferring to regard people with such problems as the victims not of their own behaviour, but of social structures and systemic failures.

In chapter 7, I introduced Charles Murray's argument that lone parents, the long-term unemployed and petty criminals together constitute an irresponsible 'underclass'. Murray explicitly makes the point that he wants 'to reintroduce the notion of blame and sharply reduce our willingness to call people "victims"' (1990: 71). His policy prescription is to roll back the welfare state. Murray's approach, however, is an extreme example and Ryan has argued that victim-blaming approaches to social problems can be much subtler than this. He characterizes the process as follows:

> First, identify the problem. Second, study those affected by it and discover in what ways they are different from the rest of us as a consequence of deprivation and injustice. Third, define the differences as the cause of the social problem itself. Finally, of course, assign a government bureaucrat to invent a humanitarian action programme to correct the differences. (1977: 66)

The policy that flows from a behavioural analysis of social problems will be one that seeks to change the behaviour of those affected and that leaves deprivation and injustice untouched. In chapter 7 I also mentioned that similar criticisms have been made of policy initiatives informed by the concept of social exclusion. In some (but by no means all) ways, the UK government's Social Exclusion Unit, established in 1997, has conducted itself just as Ryan would predict. It has identified phenomena such as rough sleeping and teenage pregnancy as problems, and then sought to devise 'joined-up' policy solutions to change the behaviour of rough sleepers and teenagers (SEU 2001).

Victim-blaming policy approaches may, for example, attribute the ill health to which poor people are subject to their unhealthy habits and unsuitable lifestyle choices. Edwina Currie, a former Conservative Health Minister in the UK, infamously blamed the high incidence of ill health in the north of England not on the higher levels of deprivation in the north compared to the south, but on the high-fat diet allegedly preferred by northerners (*The Independent*, 3 June 1988). A subsequent White Paper on health strategy made no mention of the role that poverty plays in undermining good health (see chapter 4), but stressed instead the importance of promoting healthy lifestyles and personal responsibility (DH 1992). The victim-blaming approach may also be used to excuse policy failure. Poor educational outcomes among disadvantaged minority ethnic groups may be blamed on the culture and attitudes of the children, rather than the standard and appropriateness of the teaching they have received (e.g. Law 1996: ch. 6).

It is of course possible for social policies to address structural or systemic causes of social problems. In fairness to the UK government, it has at the time of writing committed itself to tackling childhood poverty, a structural social factor that strongly correlates with the incidence of youth homelessness and teenage pregnancy (Kiernan 2002). It has acknowledged the relationship between inequality and health (Acheson 1998). And in fairness to the UK's Social Exclusion Unit, its report on truancy and school exclusion (SEU 1998) has acknowledged the racialized nature of the school exclusion process and, in particular, the self-fulfilling consequences of the stereotypical assumptions held by many teachers in relation to the behaviour and aspirations of African-Caribbean boys.

Social policies may well have redistributive effects that mitigate structural inequality (see chapter 5) or compensatory effects that mitigate systemic disadvantage (see chapter 7). But in practice they tend also to include elements that address what are identified as problematic behaviours.

Crime and Anti-Social Behaviour

The most obvious arena in which this is so is that of criminal justice policy. Criminal justice policy is not always thought of as social policy and, as we saw in chapter 1, spending on law and order is not usually counted as social spending. Criminology, therefore, is generally regarded as a separate academic subject from Social Policy. None the less, in many universities the two subjects are taught together and there is plenty of evidence of an emerging synthesis between the subjects. There are at least three good reasons for regarding Social Policy and Criminology as interrelated subjects.

First, there is the issue of community safety and the importance to human wellbeing of physical security. The criminal justice system plays an important role in providing a safe and congenial local environment in which to live. The concept of 'community safety', initially framed in the Morgan Report (Home Office 1991), captures the sense in which the criminal justice system may be thought of as an element within a holistic approach to *social* justice. Specifically, the Morgan Report suggested that crime prevention and reduction strategies should be situated within a broad social policy framework and based on local multi-agency collaboration between human service agencies. Elements of this approach were implemented in the UK from 1998 onwards, when local authorities and community-based agencies were given a role in partnership with the police in developing crime reduction and prevention strategies (e.g. Newburn 2003). It is an approach that links crime reduction and prevention to housing, public health, community education and social service issues.

The second reason that Social Policy and Criminology are coming together relates to the development of common theoretical understandings about the disciplinary effects of administrative processes and of prevailing shifts in policy. Post-structuralist analyses (Foucault 1977; Garland 1985) have contended that criminal justice systems and welfare systems were equally implicated in the development of the disciplinary techniques by which modern societies were governed. Penal and welfare institutions had certain things in common, not least the significance they attach to the surveillance of the individual human subject, and the way they succeed in stigmatizing certain social groups. However, just as social policies have been under pressure to change, so have penal policies (Garland 2001). In the USA and the UK, for example, a sense of crisis emerged from the 1970s onwards. The incidence of recorded crime was rising and neither prison nor alternative punishments seemed to be working. The essentially populist policy response has constituted what David Garland (2001) characterizes as a 'culture of control'. The new approach is characterized, on the one hand, by 'tougher' and more tightly regulated sentencing of offenders, but also by new methods in policing, based on 'zero-tolerance' of even minor offences, such as begging and anti-social behaviour. This new authoritarianism has its counterpart in certain elements of the social policy developments we have already discussed: in the shift towards 'workfare' (see chapter 4), in aspects of the treatment accorded to lone parents (see above), but also in what Pete Dwyer (2004b) has called the 'creeping conditionality' of social policy, a process that might yet extend, it has been suggested, to include the withdrawal of welfare benefits as a sanction for anti-social behaviour.

The third reason that Social Policy and Criminology need to be studied together relates to the way that both criminal justice policy and crime itself tend to bear in often disproportionate ways upon the poorest and most vulnerable in society (Cook 1997). Recent data reported by the UK government's own Social Exclusion Unit demonstrate that the country's growing prison population is characterized by alarming levels of past disadvantage, illiteracy and mental health problems: 27 per cent had been taken into public 'care' as a child; 67 per cent had been unemployed and 32 per cent had been homeless before imprisonment; 48 per cent had a reading ability below that expected of an 11 year old; 72 per cent of male sentenced prisoners were recorded as suffering from two or more mental disorders as were 70 per cent of female sentenced prisoners (cited by Prison Reform Trust 2004: 12). Policing and the criminal justice system, it may be argued, are directly implicated in a process of 'punitive segregation' (Young 1999) by which significant numbers of the most vulnerable or deprived people are physically excluded from society through periods of imprisonment. At the same time it is the residents of the poorest neighbourhoods that suffer most from crime (Pantazis 2000), and high levels of crime and anti-social behaviour within a neighbourhood may, in turn, exacerbate the process of neighbourhood exclusion (Lupton and Power 2002).

Crime and anti-social behaviour, like all social problems, are socially constructed. It is society that determines what conduct it will or will not tolerate. It is Social Policy that seeks critically to understand how such determinations are made, and what their wider implications are for human wellbeing.

Summary

This chapter has considered how the social policies with which Social Policy is concerned are involved both in defining and solving social problems. Specifically it has addressed:

- The way in which social problems are socially constructed. This has been illustrated using the contemporary examples of lone parenthood, homelessness, domestic violence and drug abuse. In each instance, the chapter has explored how the social problem came to be defined and the implications for the sometimes ambiguous form that social policies can take. From an analytical Social Policy perspective, existing social policy can sometimes be as much a part of the problem as the solution.
- The way in which the concept and the development of rights may be harnessed to address social problems. The chapter has discussed how social rights – as socially constructed rights to social protection and human services – have by and large been sidelined in favour of civil and political rights. Despite this, the idea of social rights has been used to champion the development of social policy to address social problems. The language of rights is of significant strategic importance to debates within Social Policy, but there is a risk that a rights-based approach will preclude discussion of responsibilities on the one hand and the identification of the underlying causes of social problems on the other.
- The way in which social policies may alternatively focus on the behaviour of the 'victims' of social problems, rather than on structural or systemic causes. In contrast to a rights-based approach, a victim-blaming approach to social problems is concerned to enforce responsibilities. The chapter has explained how this may justify either the retrenchment of social policy or an emphasis on interventions that seek to change individual behaviour or to promote personal responsibility. Elements of such an approach are often found alongside

approaches intended to address the consequences of social inequality, structural disadvantage or past policy failures.

- The sense in which crime and anti-social behaviour may be regarded as social problems. The chapter has argued that criminal justice policy has direct relevance for Social Policy: first, because crime undermines wellbeing; second, because in many ways criminal justice and welfare systems have developed in parallel with one another; third, because both criminal justice interventions and crime tend to be visited disproportionately on the most disadvantaged social groups.

9

How are the Times a-Changing?

I suggested in chapter 2 that Social Policy came of age as an academic subject at the beginning of an era of change and uncertainty, an era that began during the last decades of the twentieth century and through which, it may be argued, we are still living. Social Policy is not a static subject. The social policies that it studies are subject to continual upheaval and renewal. I have emphasized throughout this book how uniquely diverse Social Policy is as a subject, because of its multi- and interdisciplinary nature. In this chapter I shall emphasize how uniquely exciting the subject is because the object of study is perpetually on the move.

I shall first explain how the very foundations of the capitalist welfare state have lately come under threat. Second, I shall recount the arguments of those who suggest that the boundaries of Social Policy as a subject now need to be pushed much wider. Third, I shall outline some of the latest developments in the way that human services are being organized. Finally, I shall discuss some of the latest theories about the direction in which human society is changing.

The Crisis of Welfare

Since the 1970s, commentators of a variety of persuasions have claimed that the classic welfare state has been 'in crisis . . . under threat . . . in transition . . . resilient or robust . . . reshaped . . . refashioned . . . retrenched . . . reconstructed . . . residualized . . . rolled back . . . recast . . .

recalibrated . . . transformed . . . dismantled' (Powell and Hewitt 2002: 2). Clearly, not all these commentators can be right, but equally clearly something rather significant has been going on. This might give the impression that recent and current events are fearfully complicated. But readers who have already followed my introductory outline of the history, economics, politics and sociology of the capitalist welfare state should have little difficulty engaging with the account that follows. To explain what has been happening I shall recap certain of the key arguments introduced in previous chapters. Insofar as there has been a crisis of welfare in the developed countries of the world, it has been driven by three interlocking factors: economic instability and globalization (see chapters 3 and 5); a global shift in political orthodoxy (see chapters 2 and 6); and far-reaching social and demographic change (see chapters 7 and 8).

The economic component of the crisis is generally thought to have dated from the global oil price shocks in the early 1970s. The long-term effect of these was to undermine the system for maintaining exchange rate stability that had been established immediately after the Second World War and to make the global economy more volatile. Countries such as the UK experienced a protracted period of 'stagflation': a period of stagnant economic growth accompanied by high inflation. This, according to the Keynesian economic orthodoxy of the day, ought not to have been possible. Not only did several of the world's major economies experience difficulty in funding their welfare states but faith in the Keynesian economics that had justified such funding was shaken. The result was a shift in favour of a monetarist or neo-liberal economic orthodoxy. This has proved, so far, to be an enduring orthodoxy – not because it has been consistently observed in any technical sense (it has not) but because it has secured universal acceptance for an assumption that favours restraint in social spending.

The political component to the crisis of welfare was linked in part to the economic crisis because the ascendancy of neo-liberal economic theory reflected a wider renaissance of right-wing political thinking and of the 'New Right' (Gamble 1988). The New Right – while favouring the maintenance of a strong state capable of sustaining social order – sought to promote a free market economy by curtailing the state's provision of human services. The welfare state was seen as an impediment to economic efficiency and global competitiveness. But the political threat to the welfare state came not only from the New Right. With the emergence across the developed world of so-called 'new social movements' (or NSMs) came a mounting challenge from an entirely different direction (e.g. Scott 1990). NSMs embrace a spectrum of concerns that go beyond the limited scope of the ideological justifications that I characterized in figure 2.1 in chapter 2. They include the environmental movement and the women's movement, whose concerns I have discussed in some detail, but also the peace movement and a variety of social organizations concerned with cultural self-determination and the promotion of civil society against the power of the state. NSMs embrace a variety of concerns that often have little in common. But together they have tended to promote, on the one hand, a mistrust of centralized state power and demands for more participative forms of democracy. On the other, they have promoted forms of politics that are concerned more with identity issues and struggles for recognition. As a political force, the New Right – at least in its original guise – may or may not be spent, while NSMs, by their very nature, impact only at the margins of the established political process. None the less, each has left a legacy of signal importance for the future of the welfare state.

The social component to the crisis of welfare resulted from the accumulated effects of demographic transition and secular changes in patterns of family and household formation. The significance for the traditional welfare state was and is considerable: first, because – in the context of the economic crisis – it has put the sustainability of the welfare state into question; second, because – in the context of the political crisis – it has unsettled some of the basic premises on which the welfare state had been constructed. It is supposed that population ageing has rendered unviable the inter-generational contract on which the welfare state was originally based. The current working-age generation may not be able to afford the mounting costs of pensions, health and social care for the older generation. At the same time, it is supposed that changing familial customs and ideologies (highlighted by rising numbers of lone-parent households) has rendered unviable the traditionally gendered intra-generational contract on which the welfare state was originally based. From a New Right/neo-conservative perspective, the problem is that the welfare state has undermined traditional family values. From a feminist perspective, the problem has been the slowness of the welfare state to allow women to be properly independent from men. Either way, the welfare state is seen to be failing.

So, does this all signal the end of the road for the welfare state? Is there going to be anything worthwhile left for Social Policy to study? The answers to these questions are no, and yes, respectively. To put the crisis of the welfare state into perspective, it has been noted that in the UK 'welfare policy successfully weathered an economic hurricane in the 1970s and an ideological blizzard in the 1980s' (Le Grand 1990: 350). The growth of social spending may have been constrained, but social spending continued none the less. Ramesh Mishra (1990) has argued that once it has been established, it is difficult or impossible for a developed country to roll back its welfare state. This might be called the 'irreversibility thesis'. Alternatively, he says, though it takes time for a developed country to build up a welfare state, once it is in place it can be sustained and will continue to function with little need for further growth. This might be called the 'maturity thesis'. This is not to say that the welfare state does not adapt. Later in the chapter I shall discuss the ways in which it has been adapting to change.

In the meantime, what about claims that the welfare state is rapidly becoming a hopelessly old-fashioned relic? Should Social Policy be doing more than studying the welfare state? As the welfare state and the world around it changes, so must Social Policy.

The 'New' Social Policy

I have already made the point that Social Policy is concerned with more than social spending and the welfare state. There is, however, a particular argument that has been advanced that Social Policy needs radically to extend the range of issues that it is prepared to study. Michael Cahill in his book, *The New Social Policy*, argues for what he calls 'a social life analysis of Social Policy' (1994: 4). In the developed world our lives have for the most part changed immeasurably since the welfare state was first created. It is not that income maintenance, health provision, education and employment, housing and environmental protection, and the personal social services – all the services we discussed in chapter 4 – are no longer important; it is simply that Social Policy needs to consider all the other aspects of our lives that have a bearing on our wellbeing.

In a cash economy, in order to meet our most basic survival needs, such as food and clothing, we must go shopping (or somebody must do so on our behalf). To reach the shops, and – if we are dependent upon income from employment – to get to our places of work, we are likely to require some method of transport. Shopping and transport are relevant to several of the key concerns of Social Policy. For example, inadequate and overly expensive public transport networks can exacerbate unemployment and poverty in deprived neighbourhoods. The development of out-of-town hypermarkets accessible only to car users may threaten the survival of the local shops upon which poor and vulnerable people depend. As we mentioned in chapter 5, transport subsidies may have regressive redistributive economic effects, benefiting middle-class car owners at the expense of poorer people. Additionally, the irresponsible marketing in the shops of harmful foods and retail products is likely to have adverse consequences for public health. It is important that the standards of the food and other goods that we purchase should be regulated and that our rights as consumers should be protected (see May et al. 2001: ch. 19; Huby 2001).

We saw in chapter 8 just how important an influence the press and broadcasting media can be in shaping the policy-making agenda. In an age when there is a television in virtually every home and when the array of available news and entertainment media continue to proliferate, there are serious issues about the regulation of the mass media in the public interest (Liddiard 2003). More generally, in the information age, new information and communication technologies may, on the one hand, affect our lives in unforeseen and unwanted ways but, on the other, offer novel and effective ways of delivering essential human services (see Fitzpatrick 2003). Fundamentally, however, access to information and the means to communicate are necessary to social participation and individual wellbeing and are therefore a key concern for Social Policy.

In addition to survival needs and information needs, human beings have cultural or recreational needs. This had been recognized by early social investigators: 'for if the word recreation is taken in its proper sense as the activities whereby men and women recreate themselves, not only in body but also in mind and spirit, the consideration of what facilities are necessary for recreation involves the study of the whole question of leisure' (Rowntree and Lavers 1951: xi). It is only comparatively recently that Social Policy has once again begun to take seriously the need to study policy relating to the arts, sports and leisure facilities. Debates about how these might be funded remain contentious. In the UK, for example, the advent in the 1990s of the National Lottery as a source of funding for sport, culture and the arts has opened up a whole new area of policy debate (Liddiard 2003).

The 'new' Social Policy is therefore seeking to respond to social change by adopting a more holistic approach. Central to this process has been the rise of individual consumerism and the need to take account of the ways in which people's sense of their own wellbeing is being redefined by their role as consumers (Bauman 1998). And it is in this context that we should now return to consider the impact on mainstream human service provision.

Welfare Pluralism and New Managerialism

Human beings have always secured the things they need for their well-being from a mixture of sources and the intervention of the state, as a provider of human services, is, in historical terms, quite recent. However, one of the consequences of the crisis of the welfare state has been a shift in what is now generally referred to as the 'welfare mix' (e.g. Johnson

1987). In countries such as the UK that shift has been away from provision in the state sector in favour of more pluralistic forms of provision, involving three other 'sectors':

The informal sector. In chapter 2 I made the point that, before the advent of industrial capitalism, it was primarily families and communities that attended to human welfare needs. Before what Karl Polanyi (1944) called 'The Great Transformation' – by which social life became enmeshed or 'embedded' with the formal economy – that was pretty much all there was. With the benefit of analytical hindsight we can look back and define this as 'informal' welfare provision. And, of course, most of us continue to receive many of the day-to-day human services upon which we depend from within the families and communities in which we live. Caring for people takes place for the most part in the context of ordinary human relationships (see chapter 1 above). In the UK from the 1980s onwards, there has been a conscious attempt by policy makers to move away from the use of institutional care in the state sector and instead to make more extensive and more effective use of the informal sector to provide 'care in the community' for disabled and frail elderly people (e.g. Ungerson 2003).

The voluntary sector. If we consider once again how human services were provided before the advent of the capitalist welfare state, we must acknowledge the contribution of a diverse range of 'voluntary' organizations: churches and religious bodies; charities and philanthropic organizations; friendly societies, mutual societies and trade unions. Such organizations developed roles for themselves in the selective provision of social protection, healthcare and education. Although in time the welfare state took over many of the functions once performed by such organizations, the organizations themselves often survived, either as administrative agents acting on the state's behalf, or providing services that paralleled or supplemented those of the state sector (see chapter 6 above). What we tend in the UK to define as 'voluntary sector organizations' are defined elsewhere as 'not-for-profit organizations', 'non-governmental organizations', or 'organizations of civil society'. In the UK from the 1980s onwards, there have been moves by policy makers to make greater use of the voluntary sector as providers of services. For example, the management of substantial parts of the public housing stock has been transferred to the voluntary housing association movement. Additionally, community-based voluntary organizations are regarded as key 'partners' with central and local government in a variety of area-based social policy initiatives (e.g. Deakin 2003).

The private/commercial sector. Finally, it has always been possible for those who can afford to do so to purchase the human services they require on a commercial basis. The first schools and hospitals were private institutions. Once upon a time throughout the developed world, all medical doctors were private practitioners; anything beyond a rudimentary education had to be paid for; and social security during sickness and old age could only be purchased from private insurance companies. It was because free markets generally failed to guarantee adequate levels of protection for the population as a whole that state intervention had been seen to be necessary. None the less, economic liberals argue that, in the right circumstances, free markets in human services represent the most efficient and cost effective form of provision, provided that some kind of residual safety net is provided for those who simply cannot pay. In the UK from the 1980s onwards there were strenuous attempts to privatize social housing (through a 'right to buy' scheme for public sector tenants); to promote private pension provision (through tax incentives for personal pensions); to have many of the social and public services for which local government is responsible (including the provision of residential and domiciliary care, as well as services such as refuse collection and leisure facilities) contracted out to commercial providers; to have the ancillary services required within public sector organizations (such as cleaning, catering and buildings maintenance in hospitals and schools) similarly contracted out (e.g. Brunsdon 2003). More recently, there have been attempts to create public–private partnerships in which private sector companies are involved jointly with the state in financing public service infrastructure or in managing human service delivery.

The explicit shift to welfare pluralism and a mixed economy of welfare represented a response to the crisis of the welfare state. However, certain elements of the welfare state – especially core provision within the bedrock services of health and education, which enjoy high levels of public support (see chapter 4) – could not easily be devolved to the informal, voluntary or private sectors. The alternative response has been to reform the workings of those services that remain within the state sector. The basis for that reform has come to be known as 'New Public Managerialism' (or NPM) (Clarke and Newman 1997; Clarke 2003). In essence NPM represents an evolving doctrine that embraces a very particular set of assumptions about the nature of individual human rationality. Though there isn't space here to explore the point, principles of NPM, or elements of those principles, are now to be found, for example, in the way that the European Union has developed its 'open method of co-ordination' (see chapter 6) and in the World Bank's prescriptions for 'pro-poor governance' (see chapter 3). For now I can only illustrate the nature of NPM by outlining its implementation in the UK. I do this in box 9.1.

Box 9.1 The evolving face of new public managerialism: the process of marketization

For the purpose of *marketization*:

- It was first necessary to modify those street-level systems of public service accountability that were based on bureaucracy and professionalism (see chapter 6). This required that managers should take charge, but also that the claimants, clients, patients and pupils of the welfare state should be reconstituted as 'customers'.
- Second, it was necessary that customers should benefit wherever possible from competition and choice. One way to achieve this was through the creation of 'quasi-markets'. The National Health Service was divided up into purchasing organizations (such as health authorities, which would commission services on behalf of local people) and provider organizations (such as hospitals, which would provide those services). Funds within the education system were devolved so far as possible to individual schools, but distributed on a per capita basis according to the number of children each school could attract. In this way, hospitals were competing for contracts, and schools were competing for children.
- Third, it was necessary to create a new performance culture within the public services. Public service agencies were made subject to service level agreements. Staff were subject to performance targets. The performance of hospitals and schools could be measured and compared using performance league tables, thus providing customers with a basis upon which to choose between them.

Initially it was through the principles of NPM that policy-makers sought to make the public services more business-like. The idea was not to privatize, so much as 'marketize'. It was assumed that the disciplines that in a free market ensured efficiency, effectiveness and economy could be distilled and applied to public enterprise. More recently, however, NPM has assumed a somewhat different and more technocratic face. In the UK, under New Labour, it has been absorbed into a process of 'modernization' within the public services. There is a quite explicit attempt to make welfare state institutions function more and more as personalized rather than as public services.

In addition, therefore, to looking beyond the traditional boundaries of the welfare state, Social Policy is also now accommodating itself to the study of changing configurations of welfare provision and the

Box 9.2 The evolving face of new public managerialism: the process of modernization

- It was first necessary to modify traditional notions of democratic accountability by emphasizing the advantages of 'evidence-based policy' and the need to spread 'best practice' across the public services. In the name of pragmatism and under the slogan 'what counts is what works', key aspects of human service provision have been effectively de-politicized and turned into matters of technical or managerial judgement.
- Second, while performance targets remain very much in evidence, some of the cruder aspects of performance management have given way to subtler techniques of quality management, 'benchmarking', and the emergence of an 'audit culture', by which the functioning of public sector agencies and programmes is subject to continual or periodic scrutiny. Human service agencies, such as schools and hospitals, that fulfil closely specified performance criteria may be rewarded with greater financial autonomy.
- Third, the de-politicization of public service provision has been carried forward by an emphasis on partnerships between governmental, business and community organizations, but also on customer participation and consultative mechanisms. Such processes are ostensibly intended to empower the users of public services and to hold service providers to account. But, arguably, they may also co-opt people to a centrally determined and technically framed agenda.

changing character of the welfare state itself. Finally, however, Social Policy is engaging with theories or ideas that suggest that not only the character but also the very purpose of the welfare state is changing.

Post-Modernity and 'Risk Society'

I mentioned in chapter 3 the somewhat fatuous claim by Fukuyama (1992) that we have witnessed the end of history. It was a claim that was meant, perhaps, to sum up the idea that we now live in a post-everything society. It has been argued for some time that technologies and modes of social organization have moved on since the age of the Industrial Revolution and that we now inhabit a 'post-industrial' society (Bell 1973). Similarly, it has been said that, precisely because the welfare state ensures that our material needs are met, those of us in the developed world are part of an individualistic 'post-material' culture (Inglehart 1990), introspectively preoccupied – as I have suggested in chapter 7 – with issues of self-identity. The age of the Enlightenment and of capitalist modernity, in which liberalism vied with socialism (and supposedly won), has now given way, it is said, to an age of 'post-modernity' (Lyotard 1984). Such arguments are intended to capture something of the scale, the nature and the implications not just of the socio-economic changes but of the cultural changes that we are experiencing (e.g. Carter 1998). The problem for the developed world, some would argue, is not merely that affluence does not guarantee happiness, but that associated cultural shifts create new and different causes of ennui, dissatisfaction and anxiety (Jordan 2004).

The important question for Social Policy is what does the future hold? It is a question to which I shall turn in several quite speculative ways in chapter 10. For now, however, I want briefly to outline a particularly important argument about the nature of post-modernity – or late modernity – and its relevance for the welfare state.

Commentators such as Ulrich Beck (1992) and Anthony Giddens (1994) have characterized the society we now confront not so much as post-everything but as a 'risk society'. The argument goes more or less like this. The modern age into which the welfare state was originally born had been defined – as I have suggested in chapter 7 – by a struggle between the classes over the distribution of resources. But the resolution to the struggle that had been offered by the welfare state depended on another characteristic of modernity, namely the trust that people placed in science, technology, professional expertise, economic planning and political processes. What some would call post-modernity, it is argued, is better understood as a late or a new form of modernity, and what characterizes it is a crisis of trust. Science and technology are seen to have created new and potentially catastrophic environmental risks. Welfare professionals and experts are not necessarily beneficent providers of welfare: they are self-interested 'knaves' (Le Grand 2003); or else, as the various New Social Movements would claim, they are intrusive agents of patriarchy, racism or state control. Globalization has resulted in greater vulnerability to poverty and inequality, and to far less manageable forms of economic insecurity. Politicians are no longer in control and are no longer to be trusted. People's awareness and perception of risk has been transformed. This is risk society.

The implications for the welfare state are twofold. First, within the NPM framework that I have described, the institutions of the welfare state need procedurally to manage the risks with which they are supposed to contend (Hood et al. 2000). Second, and more fundamentally, the mission or role of the state must be adjusted. Its primary role is not the distribution of resources or to provide for people's needs. Its role is, to an extent, to mitigate risk, but also to enable people individually to manage risk. It has been argued by Nikolas Rose (1999) that this entails an advanced form of liberal governance designed to promote self-provisioning, prudentialism and an individualistic ethic of self-responsibility. These ideas are providing important new ways for Social Policy, as an academic subject, to interpret the changes that are evident within currently emerging social policies. For example, they help us to contextualize and to make sense of moves towards 'asset-based welfare' (such as the Child Trust Fund in the UK), provision for lifelong learning (to enable people to re-skill in the course of their working lives) and the promotion of 'work–life balance' (childcare facilities and employment practices that enable people more satisfactorily to combine paid employment and family caring responsibilities).

Summary

This chapter has discussed how Social Policy engages with a world that is undergoing fundamental change. It has addressed the following questions:

- How can we understand the 'crisis' to which the welfare state is supposed to have been subject over the past three decades? The chapter has considered the economic, political and social dimensions of the crisis, but has also reflected on the extent to which the welfare state has survived the crisis.
- How in a changing world might we extend the horizons of Social Policy beyond the boundaries of the welfare state to encompass *all* those aspects of social life that impact on human wellbeing? The chapter has discussed the extent to which a new Social Policy may emerge that encompasses issues to do with transport, consumption (including food policy, shopping and consumer protection) and leisure (sport, culture and the arts).
- How are we to interpret recent changes in human service provision: specifically, the shift of services away from direct state provision; and the new ways in which the services that remain within the state sector are managed? The chapter has firstly addressed the flexibility of the 'welfare mix'; the roles that can be played by the informal, voluntary and private sectors in the provision of human services; and recent shifts towards welfare pluralism. Secondly, the chapter has addressed the emergence of 'new public managerialism': a doctrine that is in

many ways revolutionizing the approach to public service provision by partially 'marketizing' provision on the one hand, and ostensibly de-politicizing it on the other.

- How could we construe the fundamental imperatives to which the welfare state must respond in the post- or late-modern world? The chapter has outlined the concept of the 'risk society' and explained how the response required of the welfare state is one that focuses less on service provision, more on risk management and, in particular, on an enabling mode of governance that promotes individual responsibility for the risks of modern life.

10

Where is Social Policy Going?

The fate of Social Policy as an academic subject is tied up with the future of the social policies that it studies. We have seen in the course of the book that this is a matter for global concern, and yet that it remains a matter of considerable uncertainty. But whatever happens, there will always be scope for the study of human wellbeing, of what it requires and how it may be promoted. In chapter 9 I discussed what has been happening in the realm of social policy making as the world about us changes. Current preoccupations appear to revolve around issues of risk on the one hand and management on the other. Taking this as a starting point, I propose in this final chapter speculatively to outline four contrasting future scenarios.

There are any number of possible scenarios for the future of the social policies that affect our wellbeing, but Social Policy is not in the business of crystal ball gazing. What it *can* do is to think through the logical possibilities. To illustrate this approach I have chosen just four scenarios. First, I consider the possibility that we shall find ways to attend to human welfare without any involvement by the state; that wellbeing will all be down to *self*-management. Second is a scenario in which social policy development becomes the strategic focus of a global struggle to contain or to supersede capitalism; the aim would be to combat the *sources* of risk. Third is a scenario in which we are destined to navigate a 'Third Way' that lies somewhere between these extremes, a way that entails some form of 'managerial state' (cf. Clarke and Newman 1997); fourth is a scenario in which we might explore new ways of negotiating (not managing) the ways in which human society interprets needs (rather than risks).

Welfare without the State?

My description in the last chapter of the way that welfare states respond to the demands of risk society suggested that this entailed a shift away from direct service provision and towards an enabling role: a role in which the state enables individuals better to manage the risks they face. It is a shift that is already visible, particularly in the welfare states of the English-speaking world. The question, however, is how far might that process go?

Critics of the process, such as Bob Jessop (2002), suggest that the transition we are witnessing involves a gradual 'hollowing out' of the role of the state. The changes I have already described are a part of that process. At the level of economic policy, the shift away from Keynesian economics has narrowed the scale of state intervention so as to focus on promoting economic competitiveness (rather than directly creating jobs, for example). At the level of welfare policy there has been downwards pressure on social spending and a shift towards 'workfare' policies. At the political level there has been a diminution in the power of the nation state. The individual is required to be self-governing, while the state is confined to a distant 'steering' role (or what Jessop calls 'metagovernance').

In theory, it may be possible for the state to all but disappear. John Rodger has argued that a future whereby 'self-organized welfare in a civil society in which state control is at "arm's length" may come to pass through sheer necessity' (2000: 188). This future may be some way off, but Rodger suggests we should take seriously the idea that the welfare state may give way to a 'welfare society'. The utopian notion of a welfare society is hardly new. In one sense, the classic Marxist vision of a Communism in which the state would eventually 'wither away' (Marx and Engels 1848) was a vision of a welfare society, albeit one that was never realized. More recently, however, it has been the New Right that laid claim to the vision, albeit in a very different sense. Peter Lilley, as a Conservative Secretary State for Social Security in the UK, deployed the expression in his 1993 Mais Lecture (see also Lilley 1998). He conveyed his ambition that the welfare state should be restrained so as to make way for a society in which individual responsibility, stable families and self-supporting communities would be restored. Lilley's call for a welfare society had a 'back to the future' ring to it, since it invoked an image of some halcyon pre-modern age in which the welfare state was supposedly unnecessary (cf. Marsland 1996).

Clearly it would be possible continually to revise the 'welfare mix' (see chapter 9) so that more and more human services were provided by the private sector. It is feasible that in developed economies *most* people could secure *most* of their needs for health and social care, education, housing and pensions through commercial providers. Opponents have long objected (e.g. Titmuss 1968) that this is a recipe for exploitation, and that the most vulnerable in society would receive poor quality services, or none at all. Neo-liberals disagree. They argue that free markets need not lead to anarchy and social injustice (e.g. Green 2003). On the contrary, they point to the arguments of Adam Smith, the eighteenth-century classical liberal whose thinking has been so influential among contemporary neo-liberal thinkers. Though Smith believed that free markets could harness the pursuit of economic self-interest (see chapter 5), he also contended that we are all of us inclined to seek the approval of others in our everyday dealings. It is this tendency, he claimed, that would promote – even in a free market economy – that sense of selfless civic duty that is necessary to produce the 'harmony of sentiments and passions' (1759: 72) on which human wellbeing depends. Zygmunt Bauman (1993) has suggested that the post-modern epoch has created a new space that is wholly appropriate for the cultivation of this kind of ethical individualism. And, as I understand the argument, it is on such individualism that the welfare society is supposed to depend.

An Anti-Capitalist Agenda

In contrast to a free market response to the challenge posed by risk society is the possibility that the world might seek to constrain capitalism and abate the risks that it generates. Contemporary Marxists cling to the belief that a humane form of capitalism is simply unachievable and, if democracy counts for anything, it must in time present a challenge to capitalism (Wood 1995). In chapter 3 I mentioned the heterogeneous global consortium that is generally known as the anti-globalization movement. It is a consortium that includes moderate international non-governmental organizations and aid agencies, bodies representing a variety of new social movements (see chapter 9) and a spectrum of radical and left-wing political groups. Between them they challenge the global ascendancy of capitalism, liberal democracy, Western culture and neo-liberal welfare theories (e.g. Amin 1997, and see Yeates 2001). Many of the key thinkers within the movement are diffident about their 'anti-globalization' tag, since it is not globalization *per se* that they oppose. Susan George, for example, has argued that '[t]his combat is really between those who want inclusive globalization based on co-operation and solidarity and those who want the market to make all the decisions'

(2001: 1). It is, in essence, an *anti-capitalist*, rather than an anti-globalization, alliance.

Alex Callinicos (2003) has identified a number of strands or varieties of anti-capitalism within the movement. Certainly, there is an anti-statist or pro-civil society element; an element favouring small-scale and local alternatives; a reformist element in favour of the re-regulation of capitalism; an autonomistic or neo-anarchistic element in favour of highly decentralized networks; and a socialist element favouring a democratically planned economy. Notwithstanding the tensions that exist within such an alliance, Callinicos has proposed an 'Anti-capitalist Manifesto' based on a transitional programme around which he believes it may be possible to mobilize a consensus within the movement. None of the individual elements of the proposed programme are of themselves new, but they represent a set of 'measures that would both offer immediate remedies and begin to introduce a different social logic' (2003: 132–9). These include a set of political, economic and legal measures that would mitigate the risks faced by poor nations in international markets, the risks faced by migrant labour and the risks that confront us all as a result of environmental degradation, militarization and the erosion of civil liberties. Specifically, there are calls for the cancellation of 'Third World' debt, the introduction of a 'Tobin Tax' on international currency transactions and the restoration of the international capital controls that had existed prior to the 1970s; the abolition of immigration controls and extension of citizenship rights based on residency; a programme to 'forestall environmental catastrophe' (focused, for example, on the global reduction of 'greenhouse gas' emissions); the dissolution of the military-industrial complex and the extension or restoration of civil liberties (including those eroded since 11 September 2001).

Additionally, however, there is a call for a commensurate set of social policy measures:

The introduction of universal basic income. The idea of a basic income (sometimes called a citizen's income or social dividend) is that every member of society should receive from the state an income sufficient for basic subsistence, leaving them free to choose whether and on what terms to engage in the labour market. It has been supported at various times by liberals (to whom it represents a way to limit the costs that employers must meet through wages) and socialists (to whom it represents a way of emancipating workers from exploitative labour). The effects of any basic income scheme would depend specifically on the adequacy of the level at which the basic income was set and on who exactly was taxed to pay for it. A generous basic income funded through progressive taxation and taxes on capital might clearly have considerable potential as an *anti*-capitalist measure, assuming that it could be promoted and implemented globally.

The reduction of the working week. Struggles at the height of the Industrial Revolution for the reduction in the length of the working day were eventually conceded because it was recognized that employees who worked for excessive periods of time ceased to be efficient. In the long-hours culture that characterizes the working environment in many developed countries, the same argument can be applied today. Reducing the average working week – say to 30 hours – would additionally be good for enhancing work–life balance and generally enhancing the quality of life. Depending on the manner of its implementation, it could also redistribute job opportunities, at both local and global levels, and limit the extent to which workers can be exploited.

The defence of public services and re-nationalization of privatized industries. Contrary to the agreement on tariffs and trade proposed by the World Trade Organization, it is proposed that human services, such as healthcare and education, should not be privatized or subject to open competition, but retained as public services. Where essential services and utilities, including water supply, transport, and so on, may have been privatized, these should be taken back into public control.

Progressive taxation to finance public services and redistribute wealth and income. The clear intention is that taxation should be used not only as a mechanism to provide collective forms of insurance against risk but also as an explicit mechanism for social redistribution (see chapter 5).

A Third Way Consensus?

At present, though both have been seriously proposed, and each has a logic of its own, neither of my first two scenarios is especially close to being realized. In the meantime, the scenario that is currently informing the development of the welfare state in several developed countries is that which is sometimes known as the 'Third Way' (Giddens 1998; Lewis and Surender 2004). The idea of a third or a middle way between capitalism and socialism is hardly new and has been applied in the past to describe a spectrum of policy approaches, from social democracy in Sweden (Childs 1936) to enlightened Conservatism in England (Macmillan 1938). The current incarnation of the Third Way – as a compromise between the 'old' social democratic left of the 1960s and '70s and the so-called 'New Right' of the 1980s and '90s – began life in the US under President Bill Clinton, continued in the UK under Prime Minister Tony Blair, but also surfaced across Western Europe in debates about 'the new centre' and 'purple coalitions' (Bonoli and Powell 2004).

The essence of the Third Way is that it has entailed centre-left governments adopting a neo-liberal economic approach, together with a 'modernizing' approach to public service delivery derived from new public managerialism (see chapter 9 above). It is an immediate response to the imperatives posed by risk society. Though we cannot be certain (and, for example, the use of the 'Third Way' label may well fall out of fashion), this approach does constitute a present scenario that could become the orthodoxy of the future. I would argue that it is not so much new as an essentially 'hybrid' approach that draws on and adapts elements from all four of the established ideological justifications that I outlined in figure 2.1 in chapter 2. Taking the UK as the current Third Way prototype, it exhibits the following elements (see Dean 2004b):

A liberal 'welfare-to-work' strategy. Central to UK social policy at the time of writing is a strategy that includes not only 'workfare' policies in the sense I discussed in chapter 4, but also policies intended to 'make work pay', principally through means-tested supplements to low wages; and policies to enhance 'work–life balance', by modest improvements to parental leave and childcare provision.

A social democratic 'redistribution by stealth' strategy. The government has ambitiously committed itself to ending child poverty within a generation. Without appearing to have raised taxes for that explicit purpose, it has quietly succeeded in redistributing resources towards poor families.

A neo-conservative 'tough on non-conformity' strategy. Tony Blair famously promised to be 'tough on crime and tough on the causes of crime' and his government has been amongst those that have implemented a shift towards a more authoritarian approach in its criminal justice policies. It is an authoritarianism that extends to aspects of its social inclusion strategies – in relation, for example, to rough sleeping and teenage pregnancy (see chapter 8).

A socially conservative 'promoting active citizenship' strategy. Allied to a desire to promote civic responsibility, to widen the welfare mix by encompassing elements of the voluntary sector, and to engage with community and faith-based organizations, the UK government has been actively encouraging citizen participation and voluntary activity.

What these elements or strands between them require is a centralized but distinctively managerial form of state power.

A Politics of Needs Interpretation

My final scenario is more tentative in nature. It is based on a sort of thought experiment, rather than the analysis of existing trends.

The first stage of the experiment requires that we think again about how to define human wellbeing. Is it to be defined negatively, in terms of the avoidance of risk; or positively, in terms of the satisfaction of need? Risks are imposed on us from without. Our needs – beyond what we require for bare physical survival – we can as human beings define for ourselves in the course of our everyday struggles to achieve a good life. In chapter 8 I drew out the distinction that can be made between rights that are imposed from above and those we may seize from below. It is through the language of rights that people have in the past been able to name and claim their needs. The risk society thesis contends that we have lost control over that process. However, it is through what Nancy Fraser has called 'a politics of needs interpretation' (1989) that we could, perhaps, reclaim it.

A politics of needs interpretation takes us beyond the parameters of the ideological justifications outlined in figure 2.1 in chapter 2. It brings the politics of identity (see chapter 7 above) into the equation. This is the second stage in the thought experiment. How might it be possible to combine struggles over the redistribution of resources with identity-based struggles for recognition? Is the old politics of social justice compatible with the politics of the new social movements? This is a continuing debate (see Fraser and Honneth 2003). For her part, however, Fraser is clear that they are parallel struggles. What this requires, she argues (see Fraser 1997), is:

- Parity of participation and an end to all systemic inequalities. Women, people of all ages and ethnicities, disabled people and members of other marginalized social groups should have an equal voice.
- The ability of these diverse publics to communicate across lines of difference. In other words, formal parity of participation is not enough: we must find ways to establish effective dialogue.
- That 'publicity' – in its literal sense – be accorded to 'private' concerns, where these are held in common. The privately experienced needs of women and of oppressed minorities, that have gone unrecognized and unmet, should be openly addressed.
- That the boundaries between state and civil society become more permeable as more open forms of democracy develop. In other words, the administrative state apparatus must become less rigid and more

directly accountable, but at the same time the institutions of civil society (such as churches and residents' associations) should not be allowed to become claustrophobic media of social regulation.

The third stage in the thought experiment is to consider how this might impact in practice on the social policy-making process. As I understand it, the politics of needs interpretation offers both an alternative strategy and an alternative ethos. At the strategic level, it provides a way for global campaigners and the users of locally provided human services to frame their demands. Rather than understanding the focus of the policy-making process as the management of risk (or as the means by which to enable people to manage their individual risks), it may be understood as a forum in which to negotiate for mutual recognition of, and collective responsibility for, individual needs.

This requires forms of participation that are driven from the bottom up, not organized from the top down. And it requires methods of communication that are genuinely inclusive. Opportunities for this kind of practical needs negotiation can be forged as much in the developing as in the developed world, albeit that at present this is generally achieved only at a local community level (see Wainwright 2003). To think laterally, however, new technologies are providing increasingly feasible mechanisms through which to establish virtual 'communication communities' (Apel 1980: 277): communities within which shared needs can be effectively identified and mutual responsibilities negotiated. Virtual communication may forge real communities, and real communities can establish effective social movements, reflecting a new kind of social policy ethos. This brings me back to an issue I touched upon in chapter 1 when I suggested that the role of Social Policy as an academic subject is to think about ethical principles. A politics of needs interpretation would be premised as much on an ethic of care as an ethic of justice. In a sense it would demand both a welfare society *and* a welfare state.

Summary and Conclusion

In this final chapter I have presented four very different scenarios for the future of social welfare or human service provision:

- One possibility is that the present tendency for welfare states to move away from direct service provision will continue. The social policy functions of the welfare state could become increasingly hollowed out, to the point where it fulfils, at most, an arm's-length enabling or steering function. It is contended by some that this would allow a 'welfare society', based on self-provisioning and civic responsibility, to function.

- An alternative possibility is that, under pressure from a global anti-capitalist movement, welfare states will in time introduce universal basic income schemes, working hours will be reduced, public service provision will be preserved and enhanced, funded through progressive taxation. It is contended by some that there will be sufficient democratic consensus at a global level to constrain the threat that capitalism poses to human wellbeing.
- A further alternative is to be found in the approach currently espoused in the developed world by certain 'Third Way' governments. This represents a compromise between competing ideological influences and embraces a complex mixture of economic liberalism, restrained social democratic tendencies, neo-conservative moral authoritarianism and social communitarianism. It may be that the future of the welfare state will continue to be defined within these broad parameters.
- The final possibility is the most speculative in that it involves a new way of thinking about social policy provision. It is suggested that through a politics of needs interpretation it would be possible to give an equal and meaningful voice in policy making to marginalized social groups and to open up a more democratic process for the recognition of human needs and the negotiation of collective responsibilities. Such ideas are by no means strategically impractical and raise important ethical issues for us to consider.

You may be asking: which scenario should we choose? Which would you or I choose? From the trail of indications I have left throughout this book you may deduce that, for my own part, I am attracted by elements of the anti-capitalist social policy agenda, but also by the idea of a politics of needs interpretation. But that is not the point. However passionately I personally might favour one scenario or oppose another, that doesn't mean there is one correct prophecy, still less that there is a single acceptable orthodoxy within Social Policy. It doesn't matter how – if at all – you would choose between these scenarios, or where your sympathies might lie, you can still study Social Policy. Studying Social Policy doesn't force you to decide, although it certainly gives you a chance to think through where you stand. Students of Social Policy are not required to be political eunuchs or neutral observers, but they *must* be prepared, *first*, to recognize and acknowledge their personal convictions, and *second*, to separate out their convictions from the rigorous analysis of alternative possibilities.

In conclusion, this has not been a definitive introduction to Social Policy. There is so much that has been left out. In any event, a truly 'scholarly' approach to Social Policy should never lay claim to be definitive. Scholarship may be regarded as a somewhat pretentious notion, but there is nothing pretentious about Social Policy as an academic subject. Students of Social Policy must accept that their understanding of how to optimize human wellbeing can never be certain or complete. But the search for such understanding, I have found, is an abiding and absorbing challenge.

References

Abercrombie, N. (2004) *Sociology*, Cambridge: Polity.

Acheson, D. (1998) *Independent Inquiry into Inequalities in Health*, London: The Stationery Office.

Ahmad, W. and Craig, G. (2003) 'Race' and 'social welfare', in P. Alcock, A. Erskine and M. May (eds), *The Student's Companion to Social Policy*, 2nd edn, Oxford: Blackwell.

Alcock, P. (1993) *Understanding Poverty*, Basingtoke: Macmillan.

Alcock, P. (2003) 'The subject of social policy', in P. Alcock, A. Erskine and M. May (eds), *The Student's Companion to Social Policy*, 2nd edn, Oxford: Blackwell.

Allsop, J. (2003) 'Health care', in P. Alcock, A. Erskine and M. May (eds), *The Student's Companion to Social Policy*, 2nd edn, Oxford: Blackwell.

Amin, S. (1997) *Capitalism in the Age of Globalization*, London: Zed Books.

Apel, K. (1980) *Towards the Transformation of Philosophy*, London: Routledge.

Atkinson, R. (2003) 'Urban policy', in N. Ellison and C. Pierson (eds), *Developments in British Social Policy 2*, Basingstoke: Palgrave.

Bacon, R. and Eltis, W. (1976) *Britain's Economic Problem: Too Few Producers*, London: Macmillan.

Baggott, R. (1998) *Health and Health Care in Britain*, 2nd edn, Basingstoke: Macmillan.

Baldock, J. (2003) 'The personal social services and community care', in P. Alcock, A. Erskine and M. May (eds), *The Student's Companion to Social Policy*, 2nd edn, Oxford: Blackwell.

Barrientos, A. (2004) 'Latin America: Toward a liberal-informal welfare regime', in I. Gough and G. Wood, with A. Barrientos, P. Bevan, P. Davis and G. Room, *Insecurity and Welfare Regimes in Asia, Africa and Latin America: Social Policy in Development Contexts*, Cambridge: Cambridge University Press.

Bauman, Z. (1993) *Postmodern Ethics*, Oxford: Blackwell.

Bauman, Z. (1998) *Work, Consumerism and the New Poor*, Buckingham: Open University Press.

Beck, U. (1992) *Risk Society: Towards a New Modernity*, London: Sage.

Bell, D. (1973) *The Coming of Post-Industrial Society*, London: Heinemann.

Beresford, P. and Turner, M. (1997) *It's Our Welfare: Report of the Citizens' Commission on the Future of the Welfare State*, London: National Institute for Social Work.

Bevan, A. (1952) *In Place of Fear*, 1978 edn, London: Quartet Books.

Beveridge, W. (1942) *Social Insurance and Allied Services*, Cmd. 6404, London: HMSO.

Bochel, C. and Bochel, H. (2004) *The UK Social Policy Process*, Basingstoke: Palgrave.

Bonoli, J. and Powell, M. (2004) 'One Third Way or several?', in J. Lewis and R. Surender (eds), *Welfare State Change: Towards a Third Way?*, Oxford: Oxford University Press.

Bookchin, M. (1991) 'Where I stand now', in M. Bookchin and D. Foreman, *Defending the Earth*, New York: Black Rose Books.

Bottomore, T. (1992) 'Citizenship and social class, forty years on', in T. Marshall and T. Bottomore (1992), *Citizenship and Social Class*, London: Pluto.

Bourguignon, F. and Morrisson, C. (2002) 'Inequality among world citizens 1820–1992', *American Economic Review*, vol. 92, no. 4, pp. 727–44.

Bradshaw, J. (2003) 'Lone parents', in P. Alcock, A. Erskine and M. May (eds), *The Student's Companion to Social Policy*, 2nd edn, Oxford: Blackwell.

Braverman, H. (1974) *Labor and Monopoly Capital*, New York: Monthly Review Press.

Brundtland, G. (1987) *Our Common Future*, Oxford: Oxford University Press.

Brunsdon, E. (2003) 'Private welfare', in P. Alcock, A. Erskine and M. May (eds), *The Student's Companion to Social Policy*, 2nd edn, Oxford: Blackwell.

Bulmer, M., Piachaud, D. and Lewis, J. (eds) (1989) *The Goals of Social Policy*, London: Unwin Hyman.

Burchardt, T., Hills, J. and Propper, C. (1999) *Private Welfare and Public Policy*, York: Joseph Rowntree Foundation.

Burchardt, T., Le Grand, J. and Piachaud, D. (2002) 'Introduction', in J. Hills, J. Le Grand and D. Piachaud (eds), *Understanding Social Exclusion*, Oxford: Oxford University Press.

Cahill, M. (1994) *The New Social Policy*, Oxford: Blackwell.

Cahill, M. (2002) *The Environment and Social Policy*, London: Routledge.
Callinicos, A. (2003) *An Anti-Capitalist Manifesto*, Cambridge: Polity.
Carter, J. (ed.) (1998) *Postmodernity and the Fragmentation of Welfare*, London: Routledge.
Cawson, A. and Saunders, P. (1983) 'Corporatism, competitive politics and class struggle', in R. King (ed.) *Capital and Politics*, London: Routledge.
Childs, M. (1936) *The Middle Way*, New Haven: Yale University Press.
Chitty, C. (2004) *Education Policy in Britain*, Basingstoke: Palgrave.
Clarke, J. (2003) 'Managing and delivering welfare', in P. Alcock, A. Erskine and M. May (eds), *The Student's Companion to Social Policy*, 2nd edn, Oxford: Blackwell.
Clarke, J. and Newman, J. (1997) *The Managerial State*, London: Sage.
Cochrane, A. (2003) 'The governance of local welfare', in P. Alcock, A. Erskine and M. May (eds), *The Student's Companion to Social Policy*, 2nd edn, Oxford: Blackwell.
Cohen, S. (1980) *Folk Devils and Moral Panics: The Invention of Mods and Rockers*, Oxford: Martin Robertson.
Coles, R. (2003) 'Young people', in P. Alcock, A. Erskine and M. May (eds), *The Student's Companion to Social Policy*, 2nd edn, Oxford: Blackwell.
Commission for the European Communities (CEC) (1993) *European Social Policy: Options for the Union*, Luxembourg: Office for Official Publications of the European Communities.
Cook, D. (1997) *Poverty, Crime and Punishment*, London: Child Poverty Action Group.
Daly, G. (1996) *Homeless: Policies, Strategies and Lives on the Street*, London: Routledge.
Daniel, P. and Ivatts, J. (1998) *Children and Social Policy*, Basingstoke: Macmillan.
David, M. (2003) 'Education', in P. Alcock, A. Erskine and M. May (eds), *The Student's Companion to Social Policy*, 2nd edn, Oxford: Blackwell.
Deacon, A. and Bradshaw, J. (1983) *Reserved for the Poor: The Means-Test in British Social Policy*, Oxford: Blackwell.
Deacon, B. with Hulse, M. and Stubbs, P. (1997) *Global Social Policy*, London: Sage Publications.
Deakin, N. (2003) 'The voluntary sector', in P. Alcock, A. Erskine and M. May (eds), *The Student's Companion to Social Policy*, 2nd edn, Oxford: Blackwell.
Dean, H. with Melrose, M. (1999) *Poverty, Riches and Social Citizenship*, Basingstoke: Macmillan.
Dean, H. (2001) 'Green citizenship', *Social Policy and Administration*, vol. 35, no. 5, pp. 490–505.
Dean, H. (2002) *Welfare Rights and Social Policy*, Harlow: Prentice Hall.
Dean, H. (2003) 'Welfare, identity and the life course', in J. Baldock, N. Manning and S. Vickerstaff (eds), *Social Policy*, 2nd edn, Oxford: Oxford University Press.

Dean, H. (ed.) (2004a) *The Ethics of Welfare: Human Rights, Dependency and Responsibility*, Bristol: The Policy Press.

Dean, H. (2004b) 'The implications of Third Way social policy for inequality, social cohesion and citizenship', in J. Lewis and R. Surender (eds), *Welfare State Change: Towards a Third Way?*, Oxford: Oxford University Press.

Dean, H. and Taylor-Gooby, P. (1992) *Dependency Culture: The Explosion of a Myth*, Hemel Hempstead: Harvester Wheatsheaf.

Denney, D. (1996) *Social Work and Social Policy*, Oxford: Oxford University Press.

Department of Health (DH) (1992) *The Health of the Nation: A Strategy for Health in England*, Cm. 1986, London: HMSO.

Doyal, L. and Gough, I. (1991) *A Theory of Human Need*, Basingstoke: Macmillan.

Dryzek, J. (1997) *The Politics of the Earth*, Oxford: Oxford University Press.

Durkheim, E. (1893) *The Social Division of Labour*, 1964 edn, New York: Free Press.

Dwyer, P. (2004a) *Understanding Social Citizenship*, Bristol: The Policy Press.

Dwyer, P. (2004b) 'Creeping conditionality in the UK', *Canadian Journal of Sociology*, vol. 25, no. 2, pp. 261–83.

Easton, D. (1965) *A Systems Analysis of Political Life*, New York: Wiley.

Elias, N. (1978) *The Civilising Process: The History of Manners*, Oxford: Blackwell.

Ermisch, J. (1990) *Fewer Babies, Longer Lives*, York: Joseph Rowntree Foundation.

Esam, P., Good, R. and Middleton, R. (1985) *Who's to Benefit: A Radical Review of the Social Security System*, London: Verso.

Esping-Andersen, G. (1990) *The Three Worlds of Welfare Capitalism*, Cambridge: Polity.

Esping-Andersen, G. (1999) *The Social Foundations of Post-Industrial Economies*, Oxford: Oxford University Press.

Esping-Andersen, G. (ed.) (1996) *Welfare States in Transition*, London: Sage.

European Commission (EC) (2001) *Joint Report on Social Inclusion*, Brussels: EU.

Falkingham, J. and Hills, J. (1995) *The Dynamic of Welfare: The Welfare State and the Life-Cycle*, Hemel Hempstead: Prentice Hall/Harvester Wheatsheaf.

Fanon, F. (1967) *The Wretched of the Earth*, Harmondsworth: Penguin.

Fevre, R. (2000) *The Demoralization of Western Culture: Social Theory and the Dilemmas of Modern Living*, New York: Continuum.

Finch, J. (1989) *Family Obligations and Social Change*, Cambridge: Polity.

Finer-Jones, C. (ed.) (2003) *Social Policy Reform in China*, Aldershot: Ashgate.

Fitzpatrick, T. (1998) 'The implications of ecological thought for social welfare', *Critical Social Policy*, vol. 18, no. 1, pp. 5–26.

Fitzpatrick, T. (2001) *Welfare Theory: An Introduction*, Basingstoke: Palgrave.

Fitzpatrick, T. (ed.) (2003) 'New Technologies and Social Policy', special issue, *Critical Social Policy*, vol. 23, no. 2.

Foucault, M. (1977) *Discipline and Punish*, Harmondsworth: Allen Lane.

Foucault, M. (1979) *The History of Sexuality*, London: Allen Lane.

Fox, W. (1984) 'Deep ecology: A new philosophy of our time?', *The Ecologist*, vol. 14, no. 5/6, pp. 194–200.

Franklin, B. (1789) 'Letter to Jean Baptiste Le Roy', in L. Lemay (ed.) (1987), *Writings*, New York: Library of America.

Fraser, D. (1984) *The Evolution of the British Welfare State*, 2nd edn, Basingstoke: Macmillan.

Fraser, N. (1989) *Unruly Practices: Power, Discourse and Gender in Contemporary Social Theory*, Minneapolis: University of Minnesota Press.

Fraser, N. (1997) *Justice Interruptus: Critical Reflections on the 'Postsocialist' Condition*, London: Routledge.

Fraser, N. and Honneth, A. (2003) *Redistribution or Recognition?* London: Verso.

Fukuyama, F. (1992) *The End of History and the Last Man*, New York: Basic Books.

Gaarder, J. (1996) *Sophie's World*, London: Phoenix.

Galbraith, K. (1992) *The Culture of Contentment*, Harmondsworth: Penguin.

Gamble, A. (1988) *The Free Economy and the Strong State*, Basingstoke: Macmillan.

Garland, D. (1985) *Punishment and Welfare*, Aldershot: Gower.

Garland, D. (2001) *The Culture of Control*, Oxford: Oxford University Press.

George, S. (2001) 'Another world is possible', *World Social Forum*, Library of Alternatives (*www.worldsocialforum.org*).

George, V. and Wilding, P. (1985) *Ideology and Social Welfare*, London: Routledge and Kegan Paul.

George, V. and Wilding, P. (1994) *Welfare and Ideology*, Hemel Hempstead: Harvester Wheatsheaf.

Geyer, R. (2000) *Exploring European Social Policy*, Cambridge: Polity.

Giddens, A. (1994) *Beyond Left and Right*, Cambridge: Polity.

Giddens, A. (1998) *The Third Way*, Cambridge: Polity.

Giddens, A. (ed.) (2001) *The Global Third Way Debate*, Cambridge: Polity.

Gittens, D. (1993) *The Family in Question*, 2nd edn, Basingstoke: Macmillan.

Glennerster, H. (1998) 'Welfare with the lid on', in H. Glennerster and J. Hills (eds), *The State of Welfare: The Economics of Social Spending*, 2nd edn, Oxford: Oxford University Press.

Glennerster, H. (2003a) 'Paying for Welfare', in P. Alcock, A. Erskine and M. May (eds), *The Student's Companion to Social Policy*, 2nd edn, Oxford: Blackwell.

Glennerster, H. (2003b) *Understanding the Finance of Social Policy*, Bristol: The Policy Press.

Goodman, A. and Webb, S. (1994) *For Richer, For Poorer: The Changing Distribution of Income in the UK*, London: Institute for Fiscal Studies.

Gough, I. (1979) *The Political Economy of the Welfare State*, Basingstoke: Macmillan.

Gough, I. (2000) *Global Capital, Human Needs and Social Policies*, Basingstoke: Palgrave.

Gough, I. (2003) 'Social Policy and Economic Policy', in P. Alcock, A. Erskine and M. May (eds), *The Student's Companion to Social Policy*, 2nd edn, Oxford: Blackwell.

Gough, I. and Wood, G. with Barrientos, A., Bevan, P., Davis, P. and Room, G. (2004), *Insecurity and Welfare Regimes in Asia, Africa and Latin America: Social Policy in Development Contexts*, Cambridge: Cambridge University Press.

Gould, A. (2001) 'Drugs and drug misuse', in M. May, R. Page and E. Brunsdon (eds), *Understanding Social Problems: Issues in Social Policy*, Oxford: Blackwell.

Gramsci, A. (1971) *Selections from the Prison Notebooks*, London: Lawrence and Wishart.

Green, D. (2003) 'The neo-liberal perspective', in P. Alcock, A. Erskine and M. May (eds), *The Student's Companion to Social Policy*, 2nd edn, Oxford: Blackwell.

Habermas, J. (1976) *The Legitimation Crisis*, London: Heinemann.

Hadley, R. and Hatch, S. (1981) *Social Welfare and the Failure of the State*, London: Allen and Unwin.

Hall, A. and Midgley, J. (2004) *Social Policy for Development*, London: Sage Publications.

Halsey, A. (ed.) (1988) *British Social Trends Since 1900*, Basingstoke: Macmillan.

Hantrais, L. (2003) 'Social Policy and the European Union', in P. Alcock, A. Erskine and M. May (eds), *The Student's Companion to Social Policy*, 2nd edn, Oxford: Blackwell.

Held, D. (1987) *Models of Democracy*, Cambridge: Polity.

Hill, M. (1997) *The Policy Process in the Modern State*, Hemel Hempstead: Prentice Hall.

Hill, M. (2003) 'Social policy and the political process', in P. Alcock, A. Erskine and M. May (eds), *The Student's Companion to Social Policy*, 2nd edn, Oxford: Blackwell.

Hills, J. (2003) 'The distribution of welfare', in P. Alcock, A. Erskine and M. May (eds), *The Student's Companion to Social Policy*, 2nd edn, Oxford: Blackwell.

Hills, J. (2004) *Inequality and the State*, Oxford: Oxford University Press.
Hirst, P. and Thompson, G. (1996) *Globalization in Question: The International Economy and the Possibilities of Governance*, Cambridge: Polity.
HM Treasury (2004a) *Budget 2004 – Prudence for a Purpose: A Britain of Stability and Strength*, HC 301, London: The Stationery Office.
HM Treasury (2004b) *Public Expenditure Statistical Analyses 2004*, London: The Stationery Office.
Hobbes, T. (1651) *Leviathan*, in R. Tuck, R. Geuss and Q. Skinner (eds) (1991), revised student edn, Cambridge: Cambridge University Press.
Hobcraft, J. (2002) 'Social exclusion and the generation', in J. Hills, J. Le Grand and D. Piachaud (eds), *Understanding Social Exclusion*, Oxford: Oxford University Press.
Hobsbawm, E. (1962) *The Age of Revolution: 1789–1848*, New York: Mentor.
Hoggett, P. (2000) 'Social Policy and the emotions', in G. Lewis, S. Gewirtz and J. Clarke (eds), *Rethinking Social Policy*, London: Sage.
Home Office (1991) *Safer Communities: The Local Delivery of Crime Prevention through the Partnership Approach*, Standing Conference on Crime Prevention, London: Home Office.
Hood, C., Rothstein, H. and Baldwin, R. (2000) *The Government of Risk: Understanding Risk Regulation Regimes*, Oxford: Oxford University Press.
Horsman, M. and Marshall, A. (1994) *After the Nation State*, London: HarperCollins.
Huby, M. (2001) 'Food and the environment', in M. May, R. Page and E. Brunsdon (eds), *Understanding Social Problems: Issues in Social Policy*, Oxford: Blackwell.
Inglehart, R. (1990) *Culture Shift in Advanced Industrial Society*, Princeton, NJ: Princeton University Press.
Jacobs, J. (1996) Review of V. George and R. Page (eds), 'Modern Thinkers on Welfare', *Journal of Social Policy*, vol. 25, no. 4, pp. 585–6.
Jessop, B. (2002) *The Future of the Capitalist State*, Cambridge: Polity.
Johnson, N. (1987) *The Welfare State in Transition: The Theory and Practice of Welfare Pluralism*, Brighton: Wheatsheaf.
Jordan, B. (2004) *Sex, Money and Power: The Transformation of Collective Life*, Cambridge: Polity.
Kelly, A. (1994) *The National Curriculum: A Critical Review*, London: Chapman.
Keynes, J. (1936) *The General Theory of Employment, Interest and Money*, London: Macmillan.
Kiernan, K. (2002) 'Disadvantage and demography – chicken and egg?', in J. Hills, J. Le Grand and D. Piachaud (eds), *Understanding Social Exclusion*, Oxford: Oxford University Press.
Lakin, C. (2004) 'The effect of taxes and benefits on household income, 2003–4', *Economic Trends*, no. 607, pp. 39–84.

Land, H. (1992) 'Whatever happened to the social wage?' in C. Glendinning and J. Millar (eds), *Women and Poverty in Britain: The 1990s*, Hemel Hempstead: Harvester Wheatsheaf.
Law, I. (1996) *Racism, Ethnicity and Social Policy*, Hemel Hempstead: Harvester Wheatsheaf.
Layard, R. (2003) *Happiness: Has Social Science a Clue?*, Lionel Robbins Memorial Lectures, London School of Economics, 3–5 March.
Le Grand, J. (1982) *The Strategy of Equality*, London: Allen and Unwin.
Le Grand, J. (1990) 'The state of welfare', in J. Hills (ed.), *The State of Welfare: The Welfare State in Britain Since 1974*, Oxford: Clarendon.
Le Grand, J. (2003) *Motivation, Agency and Public Policy: Of Knights, Knaves, Pawns and Queens*, Oxford: Oxford University Press.
Le Grand, J., Propper, C. and Robinson, R. (1992) *The Economics of Social Problems*, Basingstoke: Macmillan.
Leibfried, S. (2000) 'National welfare states, European integration and globalization: A perspective for the next century', *Social Policy and Administration*, vol. 34, no. 1, pp. 44–63.
Levitas, R. (1998) *The Inclusive Society?*, Basingstoke: Palgrave.
Lewis, J. (1992) 'Gender and the development of welfare regimes', *Journal of European Social Policy*, vol. 2, no. 3, pp. 159–73.
Lewis, J. (2001) 'Family change and lone parents as a social problem', in M. May, R. Page and E. Brunsdon (eds), *Understanding Social Problems: Issues in Social Policy*, Oxford: Blackwell.
Lewis, J. (2003) 'Feminist perspectives', in P. Alcock, A. Erskine and M. May (eds), *The Student's Companion to Social Policy*, 2nd edn, Oxford: Blackwell.
Lewis, J. and Surender, R. (eds) (2004) *Welfare State Change: Towards a Third Way?* Oxford: Oxford University Press.
Liddiard, M. (2001) 'Homelessness', in M. May, R. Page and E. Brunsdon (eds), *Understanding Social Problems: Issues in Social Policy*, Oxford: Blackwell.
Liddiard, M. (2003) 'Welfare, media and culture', in J. Baldock, N. Manning and S. Vickerstaff (eds), *Social Policy*, 2nd edn, Oxford: Oxford University Press.
Lilley, P. (1998) 'The Welfare Society – More Welfare, Less State', Demos Lecture, 3 November (*www.peterlilley.co.uk*).
Lipsey, D. (1994) 'Do we really want more public spending?', in R. Jowell, J. Curtice, L. Brook and D. Arendt (eds), *British Social Attitudes: The 11th Report*, Aldershot: Dartmouth.
Lipsky, M. (1980) *Street-Level Bureaucracy: Dilemmas of the Individual in Public Services*, New York: Russell Sage Foundation.
Lister, R. (2003) *Citizenship: Feminist Perspectives*, 2nd edn, Basingstoke: Macmillan.
Lovelock, J. (1979) *Gaia*, Oxford: Oxford University Press.
Lukes, S. (1974) *Power: A Radical View*, London: Macmillan.

Lund, B. (1996) *Housing Problems and Housing Policy*, Harlow: Longman.

Lupton, R. and Power, A. (2002) 'Social exclusion and neighbourhoods', in J. Hills, J. Le Grand and D. Piachaud (eds), *Understanding Social Exclusion*, Oxford: Oxford University Press.

Lynn, J. and Jay, A. (1984), *The Complete Yes, Minister*, London: BBC/Book Club Associates.

Lynn, J. and Jay, A. (1986/7) *Yes, Prime Minister*, Vols. I and II, London: BBC/Book Club Associates.

Lyotard, J. (1984) *The Postmodern Condition: A Report on Knowledge*, Manchester: Manchester University Press.

Macmillan, H. (1938) *The Middle Way*, London: Macmillan.

Manning, N. (ed.) (1985) *Social Problems and Welfare Ideology*, Aldershot: Gower.

Marshall, G. (1997) *Repositioning Class*, London: Sage.

Marshall, T. H. (1950) 'Citizenship and social class', in T. Marshall and T. Bottomore (1992), *Citizenship and Social Class*, London: Pluto.

Marsland, D. (1996) *Welfare or Welfare State?* Basingstoke: Macmillan.

Marx, K. (1887) *Capital*, 3 vols, 1970 edn, London: Lawrence and Wishart.

Marx, K. and Engels, F. (1848) *The Communist Manifesto*, 1970 Merit Pamphlet edn, New York: Pathfinder Press.

May, M. (2001) 'Protecting the "vulnerable": Welfare and consumer protection', in M. May, R. Page and E. Brunsdon (eds), *Understanding Social Problems: Issues in Social Policy*, Oxford: Blackwell.

May, M., Page, R. and Brunsdon, E. (eds) (2001) *Understanding Social Problems: Issues in Social Policy*, Oxford: Blackwell.

Meadows, D., Meadows, D., Randers, J. and Behrens III, W. (1972) *The Limits to Growth*, London: Pan.

Meyer, J., Boli, J., Thomas, G. and Ramirez, F. (1997) 'World society and the nation state', *American Journal of Sociology*, vol. 103, no. 1, pp. 144–81.

Miles, R. (1989) *Racism*, London: Routledge.

Millar, J. (ed.) (2003) *Understanding Social Security*, Bristol: The Policy Press.

Mills, C. Wright (1956) *The Power Elite*, New York: Oxford University Press.

Mishra, R. (1990) *The Welfare State in Capitalist Society*, Hemel Hempstead: Harvester Wheatsheaf.

Moore, J. (1989) 'The end of the line for poverty', speech to Greater London Conservative Party constituencies meeting, 11 May.

Morris, J. (2003) 'Community care or independent living?', in N. Ellison and C. Pierson (eds), *Developments in British Social Policy 2*, Basingstoke: Palgrave.

Murie, A. (2003) 'Housing', in P. Alcock, A. Erskine and M. May (eds), *The Student's Companion to Social Policy*, 2nd edn, Oxford: Blackwell.

Murray, C. (1990) *The Emerging British Underclass*, London: Institute of Economic Affairs.

Murray, R. (1989) 'Fordism and post-Fordism', in S. Hall and M. Jacques (eds), *New Times: The Changing Face of Politics in the 1990s*, London: Lawrence and Wishart.

National Economic Development Office (NEDO) (1989) *Defusing the Demographic Time-Bomb*, London: NEDO.

New Economics Foundation (NEF) (2004) *A Well-being Manifesto for a Flourishing Society*, London: NEF.

Newburn, T. (2003) 'Criminal justice policy', in N. Ellison and C. Pierson (eds), *Developments in British Social Policy 2*, Basingstoke: Palgrave.

Nussbaum, M. (2000) *Women and Human Development: The Capabilities Approach*, Cambridge: Cambridge University Press.

Offe, C. (1974) 'Structural problems of the capitalist state', in K. von Beyme (ed.), *German Political Studies*, Vol. 1, London: Sage Publications.

Offe, C. (1992) 'A non-productivist design for social policies', in P. van Parijs (ed.), *Arguing for Basic Income*, London: Verso.

Office of the High Commissioner for Human Rights (OHCHR) (2002) *Draft Guidelines: A Human Rights Approach to Poverty Reduction Strategies*, Geneva: United Nations.

Oliver, D. and Heater, D. (1994) *The Foundations of Citizenship*, Hemel Hempstead: Harvester Wheatsheaf.

Oliver, M. (2003) 'Disabled people', in P. Alcock, A. Erskine and M. May (eds), *The Student's Companion to Social Policy*, 2nd edn, Oxford: Blackwell.

Organization for Economic Co-operation and Development (OECD) (2003) *Tax Database* (*www.oecd.org*).

Organization for Economic Co-operation and Development (OECD) (2004) *Social Expenditure Database (SOCX) 1980–2001* (*www.oecd.org*).

Pahl, J. (2003) 'The family and welfare', in J. Baldock, N. Manning and S. Vickerstaff (eds), *Social Policy*, 2nd edn, Oxford: Oxford University Press.

Pantazis, C. (2000) 'Tackling inequalities in crime and social harm', in C. Pantazis and D. Gordon (eds), *Tackling Inequalities: Where are We Now and What can be Done?* Bristol: The Policy Press.

Parker, R. (1981) 'Tending and Social Policy', in E. Goldberg and S. Hatch (eds), *A New Look at the Personal Social Services*, London: Policy Studies Institute.

Parry, R. (2003) 'Social policy within the United Kingdom', in P. Alcock, A. Erskine and M. May (eds), *The Student's Companion to Social Policy*, 2nd edn, Oxford: Blackwell.

Pascall, G. (1997) *Social Policy: A New Feminist Analysis*, London: Routledge.

Piven, F. and Cloward, R. (1977) *Poor People's Movements*, New York: Pantheon Books.

Polanyi, K. (1944) *The Great Transformation*, New York: Farrar & Rinehart.
Poulantzas, N. (1980) *State, Power, Socialism*, London: Verso.
Powell, M. and Hewitt, N. (2002) *Welfare State and Welfare Change*, Buckingham: Open University Press.
Power, A. (1999) *Estates on the Edge: The Social Consequences of Mass Housing in Northern Europe*, Basingstoke: Macmillan.
Prison Reform Trust (2004) *Prison Reform Trust Factfile* (*www.prisonreformtrust.org.uk*).
Prosser, T. (1983) *Test Cases for the Poor*, London: Child Poverty Action Group.
Qureshi, H. and Walker, A. (1989) *The Caring Relationship*, Basingstoke: Macmillan.
Radford, L. (2001) 'Domestic violence', in M. May, R. Page and E. Brunsdon (eds), *Understanding Social Problems: Issues in Social Policy*, Oxford: Blackwell.
Rhodes, R. (1997) *Understanding Governance: Policy Networks, Governance, Reflexivity and Accountability*, Buckingham: Open University Press.
Ricardo, D. (1817) *Principles of Political Economy and Taxation*, 1912 edn, London: Dent.
Ritzer, G. (2004) *The McDonaldization of Society*, rev. edn, Thousand Oaks: Pine Forge Press.
Roche, M. (1992) *Re-thinking Citizenship*, Cambridge: Polity.
Rodger, J. (2000) *From a Welfare State to a Welfare Society*, Basingstoke: Macmillan.
Rogers, R. and Power, A. (2000) *Cities for a Small Country*, London: Faber and Faber.
Roosevelt, F. D. (1944) State of the Union Address to Congress, 11 January, in S. Rosenman (ed.), *The Public Papers and Addresses of Franklin D. Roosevelt*, Vol. XIII, 1950 edn, New York: Harper.
Rose, N. (1999) *Powers of Freedom: Reframing Political Thought*, Cambridge: Cambridge University Press.
Rowntree, S. B. and Lavers, G. (1951) *English Life and Leisure: A Social Study*, London: Longmans.
Ryan, W. (1971) *Blaming the Victim*, New York: Pantheon Books.
Ryan, W. (1977) 'Blaming the victim: Ideology serves the establishment', in P. Wickman (ed.), *Readings in Social Problems: Contemporary Perspectives*, New York: Harper and Row.
Sarup, M. (1993) *An Introductory Guide to Post-Structuralism and Post-modernism*, 2nd edn, Hemel Hempstead: Harvester Wheatsheaf.
Schiengold, S. (1974) *The Politics of Rights*, New Haven: Yale University Press.
Scott, A. (1990) *Ideology and New Social Movements*, London: Unwin Hyman.
Sen, A. (1985) *Commodities and Capabilities*, Amsterdam: Elsevier.

Sen, A. (1999) *Development as Freedom*, Oxford: Oxford University Press.
Sevenhuijssen, S. (2000) 'Caring in the Third Way: The relation between obligation, responsibility and care in Third Way discourse', *Critical Social Policy*, vol. 20, no. 1, pp. 5–37.
Smith, A. (1759) *The Theory of Moral Sentiments*, 1976 edn, Indianapolis: Liberty Fund.
Smith, A. (1776) *An Inquiry into the Nature and Causes of the Wealth of Nations*, 1900 edn, London: George Routledge.
Snow, C. P. (1964) *The Corridors of Power*, 2000 edn, Thirsk: House of Stratus.
Social Exclusion Unit (SEU) (1998) *Truancy and School Exclusions*, London: Cabinet Office.
Social Exclusion Unit (SEU) (2000) *Minority Ethnic Issues in Social Exclusion and Neighbourhood Renewal*, London: Cabinet Office.
Social Exclusion Unit (SEU) (2001) *Preventing Social Exclusion: Report by the Social Exclusion Unit*, London: Cabinet Office.
Sparkes, J. and Glennerster, H. (2002) 'Education's contribution', in J. Hills, J. Le Grand and D. Piachaud (eds), *Understanding Social Exclusion*, Oxford: Oxford University Press.
Squires, P. (1990) *Anti-Social Policy: Welfare, Ideology and the Disciplinary State*, Hemel Hempstead: Harvester Wheatsheaf.
Standing, G. (2002) *Beyond the New Paternalism*, London: Verso.
Taylor, D. (1998) 'Social identity and social policy: Engagements with post-modern theory', *Journal of Social Policy*, vol. 27, no. 3, pp. 329–50.
Taylor-Gooby, P. (2002) 'The silver age of the welfare state: Perspectives on resilience', *Journal of Social Policy*, vol. 31, no. 4, pp. 597–621.
Thane, P. (1982) *Foundations of the Welfare State*, Harlow: Longman.
Thatcher, M. (1995) *The Downing Street Years*, London: HarperCollins.
Timmins, N. (2001) *The Five Giants: A Biography of the Welfare State*, rev. edn, London: HarperCollins.
Titmuss, R. (1955) Lecture at the University of Birmingham in honour of Eleanor Rathbone, reproduced in P. Alcock, H. Glennerster, A. Oakley and A. Sinfield (eds) (2001), *Welfare and Wellbeing: Richard Titmuss' Contribution to Social Policy*, Bristol: The Policy Press.
Titmuss, R. (1968) *Commitment to Welfare*, London: Allen and Unwin.
Titmuss, R. (1970) *The Gift Relationship*, London: Allen and Unwin.
Townsend, P. (1979) *Poverty in the UK*, Harmondsworth: Penguin.
Townsend, P. and Gordon, D. (eds) (2002), *World Poverty: New Policies to Defeat an Old Enemy*, Bristol: The Policy Press.
Turner, B. (1986) *Citizenship and Capitalism: The Debate over Reformism*, London: Allen and Unwin.
Turner, B. (1990) 'Outline of a theory of citizenship', *Sociology*, vol. 24, no. 2, pp. 189–217.

Ungerson, C. (2003) 'Informal welfare', in P. Alcock, A. Erskine and M. May (eds), *The Student's Companion to Social Policy*, 2nd edn, Oxford: Blackwell.

United Nations Development Programme (UNDP) (1997) *Human Development Report 1997*, Oxford: Oxford University Press.

United Nations Development Programme (UNDP) (2000) *Human Development Report 2000*, Oxford: Oxford University Press.

United Nations Development Programme (UNDP) (2001) *Human Development Report 2001*, Oxford: Oxford University Press.

United Nations Development Programme (UNDP) (2003) *Human Development Report 2003 – Millennium Development Goals: A Compact among Nations to End Human Poverty*, New York: Oxford University Press.

United Nations Human Settlements Programme (UN-HABITAT) (2003) *The Challenge of Slums – Global Report on Human Settlements 2003*, London: Earthscan.

Wainwright, H. (2003) *Reclaim the State: Experiments in Popular Democracy*, London: Verso.

Walker, A. (1984) *Social Planning*, Oxford: Blackwell.

Walker, A. and Maltby, T. (2003) 'Older people', in P. Alcock, A. Erskine and M. May (eds), *The Student's Companion to Social Policy*, 2nd edn, Oxford: Blackwell.

Weber, M. (1914) *Economy and Society*, 1968 edn, New York: Bedminster.

Wells, H. G. (1909) *Ann Veronica: A Modern Love Story*, 1969 edn, Harmondsworth: Penguin.

Wilensky, H. (1975) *The Welfare State and Equality: Structural and Ideological Roots of Public Expenditure*, Berkeley: University of California Press.

Wilkinson, R. (1996) *Unhealthy Societies: The Afflictions of Inequality*, London: Routledge.

Williams, F. (1989) *Social Policy: A Critical Introduction*, Cambridge: Polity.

Wilson, W. (1987) *The Truly Disadvantaged*, Chicago: Chicago University Press.

Wood, E. Meiksins (1995) *Democracy Against Capitalism: Renewing Historical Materialism*, Cambridge: Cambridge University Press.

World Bank (2001) *World Development Report 2000/2001*, Oxford: Oxford University Press.

Yeates, N. (2001) *Globalization and Social Policy*, London: Sage Publications.

Young, J. (1999) *The Exclusive Society*, London: Sage Publications.

Index